Rewiring the Spirit

Rewiring the Spirit

Neuroplasticity and Spiritual Growth

Aisha Calderon

Mindful Pages

Published in 2026

ISBN: 9789375369455 (PB)
ISBN: 9789375362944 (eBook)

Published by

Mindful Pages
Imprint of Alpha Editions LLC
312 W. 2nd St #1834
Casper, WY 82601, USA

This book was developed using advanced writing tools to support the drafting and ideation process. All content has been thoughtfully curated, refined, and reviewed to ensure quality and relevance.

Content

Introduction

On certain mornings you wake and sense, before thought fully forms, a faint misalignment between the life you are living and the life you suspect might be possible. Nothing is obviously wrong. The people you love are still there. Your responsibilities have neither grown nor shrunk. You respond to messages, attend the meeting, make the dinner, hold the conversation. Yet something inside feels slightly out of tune, as though a quiet, persistent chord is vibrating against the grain of the day. You swallow the feeling, as most adults do, and tell yourself you are simply tired. But it returns, often at the least convenient moment, with that curious mixture of restlessness and longing that is difficult to name and even harder to soothe.

From time to time you try to address it. You pick up a meditation app, hoping ten minutes of mindful breathing might soften the edges. You begin a gratitude notebook because a speaker claimed it would "rewire" your mindset. A podcast on resilience fills the commute with polished advice. For a few days—sometimes even a fortnight—you feel lighter, steadier, faintly renewed. Then something small derails you: an offhand criticism, a stressful email, the news cycle howling with its latest catastrophe. Suddenly the old reactions return in full force, as though the brief period of clarity never happened at all. You feel exasperated with yourself. Why do insights fade so quickly? Why do good intentions evaporate under pressure? Why does change, so earnestly desired, refuse to hold?

This book begins precisely in that gap between aspiration and endurance. Many people today feel spiritually hungry without considering themselves religious, psychologically overloaded without identifying as ill, morally uneasy without believing they are bad. They live in a world brimming with information yet thin on wisdom, a world that promises self-improvement while delivering constant distraction. The result is a peculiar tension: we know more than ever about the mind, yet we struggle to inhabit our own inner lives with calm, compassion, and clarity. This tension is not a personal failing. It is a wiring issue.

For much of human history, language about inner transformation has been cloaked in metaphor—heart, soul, spirit, enlightenment, awakening. These terms have shaped civilisations and comforted generations, yet they often float free from the material realities of our bodies. At the same time, the modern cognitive sciences have illuminated how the brain forms habits, stores memories, decodes threats, and learns new responses. What has been strangely missing is a conversation between these worlds. Spiritual traditions offer powerful practices but sometimes lack clear explanation of why they work. Neuroscience offers rich explanation but often lacks guidance on how to live. This book bridges that divide by treating spiritual growth not as a mystical exception to human biology but as a disciplined conversation with it.

Rewiring the Spirit proposes a simple but profound idea: that the qualities long associated with spiritual maturity—patience, empathy, courage, gratitude, presence—are not vague ideals but trainable traits rooted in the brain's plasticity. Neuroplasticity is the brain's ability to change its structure and function in response to repeated experience. It is continuous, non-negotiable, and astonishingly democratic. Every breath taken with awareness, every pause before reacting, every small act of kindness initiates micro-adjustments in neural circuitry. These changes are usually imperceptible in the moment, which is why transformation so often feels elusive. But they accumulate. Tiny strands of neural fibre begin to strengthen, forming new routes through which attention, emotion, and choice can travel. Under stress, the old pathways may still dominate—at first. But with consistent practice, the balance of power begins to shift.

Understanding this—truly understanding it—changes the entire landscape of spiritual life. It removes transformation from the realm of wishful thinking and places it squarely in the domain of learnable skill. It reframes failure not as moral weakness but as predictable neural regression. It encourages humility, not because growth is impossible, but because it is incremental, embodied, and often quietly won. Above all, it restores agency. If the brain is still shaping itself, then each day provides an opportunity—not guaranteed, but real—to influence who we are becoming.

Yet this is more than a book about the brain. It is a book about the human spirit: that elusive, stubborn sense that life ought to mean more than survival; that we are called to a deeper quality of presence; that compassion is not merely pleasant but necessary for human flourishing. Spiritual growth has always concerned itself with what kind of person one becomes—how one sees the world, treats others, and responds to suffering. But too often the discussion drifts into abstraction or moralising. What we need is a grounded, practical understanding of how inner change actually takes root.

When viewed through the lens of neuroplasticity, many long-standing struggles begin to make sense. The reason a single argument can erase weeks of calm is that older, threat-based circuits fire faster and more forcefully than newer, reflective ones. The reason shame lingers is that the brain encodes social pain with unusual tenacity. The reason we revert to familiar patterns—even miserable ones—is that habit loops are efficient and the brain prefers efficiency over novelty. None of this is destiny. It is merely the starting point from which transformation proceeds. But acknowledging these forces helps rebalance the fight. You stop blaming yourself for what is, in truth, a natural consequence of how the nervous system evolved to protect you.

The stakes, both personal and societal, are considerable. We are living through a period of chronic overwhelm: news that agitates, technologies that fragment attention, workplaces that reward relentless output, and cultural currents that amplify outrage. The nervous system, designed for brief dangers and long recoveries, is being asked to operate under near-constant strain. We should not be surprised if many feel spiritually exhausted or psychologically depleted. Nor should we mistake this exhaustion for purely individual weakness. It is a predictable response to an environment that keeps tugging us back into survival mode.

Against this backdrop, the practices explored in the chapters ahead—meditation, compassion, gratitude, habit redesign, narrative reframing—are not feel-good exercises. They are acts of reclamation. They help return the nervous system to a more expansive mode in which reflection, connection, creativity, and meaning can emerge. They cultivate the inner spaciousness required for courage. They temper reactivity so that choice becomes possible where compulsion once reigned. They are not quick fixes, nor are they guaranteed. But they are reliable tools, shaped by centuries of spiritual inquiry and now increasingly understood by science.

Consider meditation. It is often marketed as a relaxation technique, a soothing pause in a stressful day. But its deeper function is far more demanding and transformative. It retrains attention itself: the fundamental mechanism through which reality is perceived, beliefs are maintained, and behaviour is initiated. To sit with the breath is to practise returning—again and again—to the place from which all perception begins. Each return is a subtle act of resistance against distraction; each moment of awareness is a small vote for clarity over chaos. In the long run, these micro-choices sculpt the neural foundations of equanimity.

Compassion, too, is more biological than we tend to assume. Human beings are wired to connect, yet modern life often frays these circuits through isolation, conflict, and unrelenting self-judgement. Compassion practice is not sentimental optimism; it is a disciplined reorientation of the social brain. When one quietly wishes another person well, especially in moments of tension, something shifts. The defensive posture softens. The nervous system receives a signal of safety. The world feels less adversarial, and responses become less reactive. This is not mystical. It is neurobiological training disguised as kindness.

Gratitude, perhaps the most underestimated of all spiritual practices, counterbalances the brain's natural bias for threat. It teaches the mind to widen its field of view, to notice what is steady and supportive alongside what is urgent or distressing. This shift is subtle but potent, especially over time. It is not about forced positivity. It is about recalibrating attention so that life is experienced in fuller, richer proportion. What begins as a deliberate exercise can eventually become a habitual lens.

But growth is never linear. Trauma leaves its own signatures in the brain, creating loops of anticipation, hypervigilance, or numbness. Old stories—about failure, guilt, unworthiness—embed themselves in memory networks and shape perception long after the original events. Even earnest practice can feel futile during seasons of emotional turbulence. Understanding these patterns is itself a form of compassion. It allows us to meet our own resistance with patience rather than frustration. It also highlights the necessity of honest mapping: noticing the triggers, stories, and bodily responses that define our personal wiring. Without such clarity, attempts at transformation often hover above the surface of life, disconnected from the deeper currents that govern behaviour.

In this exploration, community matters. The brain is deeply social; it reshapes itself through every interaction, every conversation, every shared ritual. For that reason, spiritual growth cannot be entirely solitary. Healthy communities provide coherence, safety, and inspiration. Unhealthy ones tighten the grip of fear, compliance, and dependency. Navigating this distinction requires both discernment and humility. It also requires an appreciation of how group dynamics influence neural pathways as surely as personal practice does.

A consistent theme throughout this book is that transformation thrives not through heroic effort but through sustained, modest action. Spiritual traditions have always emphasised discipline, yet the form this discipline takes is often misunderstood. It is not about willpower alone. It is about designing rhythms that support the nervous system rather than strain it. It is about creating environments that nudge attention towards what matters. It is about small micro-shifts—five minutes less scrolling, a single compassionate breath, a quiet moment of gratitude—that gradually reweight the script of one's life.

The recurrent motif you will encounter in these pages is the interplay between pathways and possibilities. Neural pathways determine what feels natural; spiritual possibilities determine what feels meaningful. Growth occurs when these two begin to converge. When calm no longer feels like a performance but a resting state. When compassion becomes the default rather than the exception. When gratitude arises spontaneously, not as a forced exercise. When attention steadies enough for insight to reveal itself. None of these shifts announce themselves dramatically. They accumulate slowly, as subtle as moss growing on stone. But over months and years they can fundamentally reorient the inner landscape.

This book is not a manual promising quick transformation. It is an invitation to engage with your own mind as both student and sculptor. It will ask you to examine long-held assumptions about who you are and how change occurs. It will encourage you to approach the workings of your nervous system with both curiosity and respect. It will insist that spiritual growth is less about transcending the body than working with it. And it will propose that every moment—pleasant or painful—is part of the training ground in which new wiring can emerge.

So the questions ahead are both practical and profound. What if your attention could be retrained to serve your deepest values rather than your default anxieties? What if compassion were not a lofty ideal but a biological skill that can be strengthened? What if gratitude, practised consistently, could alter the emotional climate of your days? What if the stories you tell about your past are not fixed verdicts but editable interpretations? What if your future self is not a fantasy but a direction of travel, shaped by the choices you make in the next five minutes?

These questions are deliberately unsettling, because true transformation always carries a gentle provocation: the suggestion that life could be lived differently. Not perfectly. Not without pain. But differently—more spaciously, more wisely, with greater steadiness and kindness. The pages ahead will not promise instant relief. What they offer instead is something more durable: a map for retraining the very circuits through which you meet the world.

The restlessness that brought you to this book is not a flaw. It is a signal. It is the brain's quiet recognition that the old pathways, though familiar, no longer suffice. It is the spirit's way of whispering that another mode of being is possible. This work will not be easy. But if you are willing to experiment—patiently, persistently, with humility—then change can take root. And in time, the qualities you once glimpsed only briefly may become steady companions.

The journey begins not with certainty but with curiosity. What might become possible if you learned to shape the wiring beneath your thoughts, your reactions, your choices? The chapters that follow will explore this question with both rigour and reverence. They will ask you to look carefully at the architecture of your mind and to participate in its remaking. They will guide you through practices that are ancient yet grounded in modern science. And they will invite you, gently but firmly, to consider that the person you long to be is not an illusion but an emerging pattern—one that can be strengthened, strand by strand, through the deliberate cultivation of attention, compassion, gratitude, and meaning.

Let us begin.

Chapter 1
The Brain That Longs for More

There is a moment familiar to many adults: standing at a kitchen sink, or pausing at a red light, when an unexpected thought flickers across the mind—*surely there is more to me than this.* It is not dissatisfaction exactly, nor is it melodrama. It is a quiet intuition that our reactions, our habits, even our ways of seeing the world might not be final truths about who we are, but merely familiar grooves worn into place. You may notice it after repeating the same argument with your partner, or hearing your own voice tighten in a meeting before you realise you are speaking. Even as the behaviour unfolds, another part of you watches with faint disbelief: *why am I doing this again?* This puzzled self, this observer who suspects that something better is within reach, is not evidence of failure. It is evidence of possibility.

For centuries, spiritual traditions have spoken to this sense that human beings are unfinished. They have insisted that the mind can be trained, the heart softened, the spirit renewed. Yet many people today feel caught between aspiration and inertia. They want to be calmer, less defensive, more present, more courageous, more compassionate. They read books, listen to podcasts, dabble in meditation or prayer. And then, in moments of pressure, they snap back to old patterns with astonishing speed. It feels as though the deeper self—the one capable of growth—keeps being dragged back by something older, heavier, and stubbornly automatic.

At the heart of this tension lies the question that opens this chapter: *What kind of brain does a human being actually have?* Is it rigid or flexible? Does early experience determine everything, or is there genuine room for transformation in adulthood? Those questions are not academic curiosities; they form the foundation of whether change is a pipe dream or a practical undertaking. And the science, surprisingly perhaps, leans towards hope.

The human brain is often described as the most complex object in the known universe, yet it is also profoundly practical. It is engineered to learn from experience—with a ruthless emphasis on efficiency—and it reorganises itself to make repeated behaviours easier. This property, known as neuroplasticity, is not a specialist function. It is the default. It governs how we learn a new language, adapt to a changed routine, recover from adversity, and develop identities that feel both deeply personal and strangely automatic. The brain does not simply store information. It *adapts*, sculpting itself according to what we pay attention to and what we practise. Which means that the person you become is not merely the result of your past. It is also the result of your habits in the present.

Consider something deceptively simple: taking a new route to work. The first morning, your mind strains as though navigating a foreign landscape. You turn too early, overshoot a corner, hesitate at junctions. But within a week the journey becomes easier. A fortnight later you can drive it while thinking about dinner. Nothing about the road changed. *You* changed—the networks responsible for spatial memory and motor planning strengthened through repetition, while the old route's pathways began to fade. This ordinary experience contains an extraordinary truth: even in adulthood, the brain is not fixed. It is a system of probabilities, not certainties; tendencies, not inevitabilities. And that fact alone reshapes the entire conversation about spiritual growth.

But plasticity cuts both ways. The same mechanism that allows you to learn a new route can also entrench old emotional patterns. If you rehearse self-criticism ten times a day, your brain will optimise for it. If you spend hours scanning for threats—real or imagined—your nervous system will become exquisitely skilled at vigilance. If your attention habitually returns to grievances, anxieties, or imagined catastrophes, the circuits associated with them will strengthen. The brain is loyal to what you practise, not necessarily to what you value.

This raises a fascinating tension at the heart of human experience. Beliefs, far from being abstract ideas, exert a literal influence on brain wiring. What you assume to be true about yourself—*I'm never good enough*, *I always mess things up*, *people don't really like me*—shapes the neural routes your mind travels every day. Attention is the sculptor. It determines which networks fire together and, over time, fuse into stable patterns. This is why spiritual traditions place such importance on reflection, contemplation, and the deliberate reorientation of thought: they understood intuitively what neuroscience now confirms, that the direction of attention slowly becomes the architecture of the self.

Imagine someone called Mara. For years, her mind has run on a single, well-worn script: *I should have done better.* Whether at work, with friends, or even alone in the quiet of the evening, her inner voice delivers a constant commentary of criticism. It feels natural, almost responsible. Then she begins a brief daily practice: before bed, she spends five minutes acknowledging one thing she handled with care that day. At first it feels artificial, almost embarrassing. But the act of attention—of noticing something she did well—begins to fire a new pattern. Over weeks, the inner critic's monologue grows less automatic. A warmer voice begins to appear, hesitant but sincere. She has not lied to herself or forced positivity; she has simply given her brain a new direction in which to grow.

This chapter explores how such shifts happen. It examines why certain patterns feel unavoidable, how old emotional reflexes cling to relevance, and why even the most earnest efforts can falter under pressure. Much of the answer lies in the brain's ancient threat systems, primed to detect danger with remarkable sensitivity. When activated, these systems narrow perception, accelerate judgement, and flood the body with urgency. In a meeting, for example, a colleague's curt comment can send someone spiralling into defensiveness before they consciously register the emotion. Their nervous system has leapt into survival mode, convinced—however irrationally—that reputation, belonging, or security is at stake. In that state, reflective thinking collapses. Empathy shrinks. Curiosity disappears. The world reduces to a binary: *attack or retreat.*

Yet the brain also possesses networks designed for reflection, empathy, and meaning-making. These systems support the broader, slower modes of perception in which nuance becomes visible and options multiply. When these networks engage, someone in the same tense meeting might feel the upward tug of defensiveness but pause long enough to recognise it. They might breathe, soften their posture, ask a clarifying question rather than assume intent. The situation does not magically improve, but it no longer dictates their entire internal landscape. This is meaning mode in action: a wider frame of awareness that changes both perception and response.

The modern world, with its constant stimulation and ambient anxiety, keeps many people locked in survival mode far more often than is healthy. And because neuroplasticity never sleeps, the more we operate from threat-based patterns, the more entrenched they become. This is why understanding the brain is not a cold scientific detour from spiritual life; it is a vital companion. Without it, we mistake automatic reactions for moral failure. We imagine ourselves stuck because we do not understand the machinery of change. We attempt transformation through sheer willpower, unaware that our practices are competing against well-established neural habits.

Spiritual traditions have always spoken of the heart, the soul, or the inner life as something malleable. Neuroscience gives us the mechanisms. When someone begins a simple breathing practice—say five minutes of noticing the inhale and exhale—they will almost certainly find their mind wandering. They may assume they are bad at meditation or unsuited to it. But if they understand that the wandering is not failure but the brain's habitual momentum, the experience takes on a different meaning. Each time they gently return to the breath, they are redirecting the loop, strengthening a circuit of awareness over reactivity. Progress is invisible moment to moment, but cumulative. Like lifting small weights each day, the strength builds slowly until one day the person realises their attention is steadier, not because life has become easier, but because the brain itself has changed.

This chapter asks a simple yet profound question: *What if the brain is not the obstacle to spiritual growth but its primary instrument?* To explore this, we will examine how neural pathways are formed, reinforced, or weakened; how beliefs and attention serve as the architects of these pathways; how survival mode competes with meaning mode; and why spiritual practices gain power when understood through the lens of plasticity. The goal is neither to reduce spirituality to biology nor to dilute science with mysticism. It is to show that the two, when brought into dialogue, illuminate each other.

The brain is not just a container for thoughts. It is a living system that longs—quietly, persistently—for coherence and meaning. It is capable of defending old habits with fierce tenacity, yet also capable of profound renewal. In the chapters ahead, we will see how this renewal unfolds through practices that are deceptively simple yet remarkably demanding: paying attention to the present moment, softening the inner critic, noticing small acts of goodness, interpreting stressful events with nuance, and gradually reshaping the stories we tell about the past.

Before those practices can take root, we must understand the terrain in which they operate. This chapter is the map. It lays out the forces that shape our reactions, the biases that direct our attention, and the biological legacies that still govern much of our modern behaviour. But it also reveals the hidden openings—those moments of choice, however fleeting—through which change begins.

As we step into the first layer of this exploration, hold this central idea: you are not imprisoned by your current wiring. You are influenced by it, certainly. Sometimes constrained by it. But the very structure of your brain is designed to be reconfigured through experience. The longing you feel for a calmer, clearer, more compassionate life is not wishful. It is a signal that your neural pathways are ready for new direction.

The next pages will show how to understand these pathways, how to work with them rather than against them, and how to recognise the subtle signs that change is already underway. The brain that longs for more is not asking for perfection. It is asking for participation. Let us begin to explore what that means.

The Plastic Brain

In October 1963, at University College London, Jerzy Konorski stood before a small audience of neurologists and proposed what many considered a provocative idea: the adult brain, long assumed to be largely immutable, might still be capable of structural change. Konorski, a Polish neurophysiologist known for his meticulous experiments on conditioned reflexes, argued that repeated patterns of activity did not merely pass through the brain—they altered it. The suggestion ran against the prevailing belief that neural wiring solidified in childhood and declined thereafter. Yet Konorski insisted that the brain's architecture remained open to revision, subtly reshaping itself each time a person learned, remembered, or adapted. For decades the claim sat at the margins of mainstream science, regarded as an intriguing but unproven speculation. It is striking, then, how thoroughly his thesis has since become consensus.

The modern term for this capacity is *neuroplasticity*, a word that sounds technical but refers to a remarkably simple truth: the brain is built to change. This is not metaphor. It is observable in microscopy, measurable in behaviour, and increasingly traceable in long-term population studies. A taxi driver learning dozens of backstreets, a violinist adapting her shoulder movements after injury, a multilingual child selecting the right word from the wrong tongue—each act leaves a physical imprint. Circuits strengthen in some places and weaken in others. The motif is clear: repetition leaves tracks.

Everyday life provides its own modest demonstrations. Consider a routine as mundane as taking a new route to work. On Monday you set off with determination, only to overtake your turning, misjudge a junction, or circle an unfamiliar roundabout. On Wednesday the path still feels uncertain, demanding constant vigilance. Yet by the second week a quiet shift occurs. Landmarks register without effort. The hands steer almost automatically. The hesitations fade. The brain has been rehearsing a sequence: visual cues, spatial judgments, motor adjustments. With each repetition, the neural pathways that support this sequence fire in tighter synchrony. Their connections strengthen. By contrast, the pathway governing your old commute, once used daily, becomes less active. Activity-based weakening—scientifically termed *long-term depression*—takes hold. The contrast between the two routes offers a simple demonstration of a profound principle: what is practised grows; what is neglected dwindles. Five words capture the core: *Repetition sculpts structure over time.*

The scientific account of this process is well established. Long-term potentiation, first observed by Terje Lømo in 1966 at the University of Oslo, describes how repeated firing between neurons increases the efficiency of their communication. Synapses become more responsive. The electrical and chemical signals that pass between cells meet less resistance. The brain becomes faster at performing the practised task. This same mechanism underlies skills far more intricate than navigating backstreets: speaking a new language, mastering a piece of music, or forming a habit of checking your phone each time it vibrates. The act of rehearsal alters the ease with which a behaviour emerges.

Yet it is important to recognise the limits alongside the possibilities. Neuroplasticity is not boundless magic. It operates under constraints: genetics, age-related changes, and the stubborn influence of earlier learning. For instance, the capacity of stroke survivors to recover function varies widely and is shaped by the severity and location of damage. Some regain fluent movement; others reach a plateau despite months of rehabilitation. Far from undermining the principle of plasticity, such outcomes emphasise its nuance. The brain is adaptable, but its adaptations are shaped by what is available—remaining circuits, pre-existing habits, and the surrounding environment. Plasticity works with the material at hand, not from a blank slate.

This interplay between capacity and constraint becomes clearer when comparing different communities. In 2000, Eleanor Maguire and colleagues at University College London published a landmark study examining the hippocampi of London taxi drivers. These drivers had spent years memorising "The Knowledge", a vast catalogue of some 25,000 streets. Maguire found that the posterior hippocampus, a region linked to spatial memory, was significantly enlarged compared with that of control participants. Place, date, and measurable change formed a coherent picture: sustained practice reshapes structure. Yet the same research noted a trade-off. The anterior hippocampus, associated with more general memory tasks, was smaller in taxi drivers. Plasticity, it seems, reallocates resources rather than expanding them indefinitely. What grows may do so at a cost.

These examples point to a central implication. The brain does not simply absorb experience; it commits to patterns. When a pathway is used consistently, the cells along it increase their communication.

When a pathway is ignored, the connections loosen. In ordinary life this principle operates quietly but relentlessly. A person who habitually checks their phone the moment a notification appears is rehearsing a loop of attention capture. A person who ruminates each night about perceived failures is practising a particular pattern of emotional interpretation. A person who takes a moment each morning to observe their breath is training an entirely different set of circuits—ones concerned with steadiness and regulation rather than speed and vigilance. The brain records each rehearsal, strengthening whichever pattern dominates.

This is why the motif of a path, quietly repeated, proves useful. A forest path widens as more travellers use it; the undergrowth returns if they stop. Similarly, neural pathways depend on use. When memories, beliefs, and reflexes are revisited, the paths between neurons widen through biological reinforcement. When they are neglected, competing paths have a chance to flourish. This is not a metaphor stretching beyond itself; it is an image rooted in a measurable process detectable in functional MRI studies and behavioural tracking.

Plasticity becomes more intriguing when considering beliefs. A belief is not a free-floating proposition. It is sustained by recurrent patterns of attention. If someone assumes that colleagues distrust them, they will scan conversations for subtle slights. Each perceived cue triggers a micro-cycle of worry, which rehearses the belief further. Their brain becomes skilled at interpreting events through that lens. This is plasticity at work: a cognitive habit strengthens the circuits that make the habit feel inevitable. By contrast, when someone begins to question a limiting belief, perhaps after an honest conversation or a moment of insight, they interrupt the old pathway. That interruption—brief though it may be—creates an opening for a new route. Repetition is required to stabilise it. But the route exists.

A counter-example illustrates the point. Some personality traits appear stable across decades. Longitudinal studies, such as those summarised by Roberts and DelVecchio (2000), show that adults tend to maintain relative consistency in traits like introversion or conscientiousness. Critics sometimes cite this stability as evidence that deep neural change is limited. Yet stability does not contradict plasticity. It simply reflects persistent reinforcement. If someone behaves in a consistently organised way for twenty years, their brain will naturally favour the circuits that support organisation. That does not mean change is impossible; it means change requires considerable, sustained practice to overcome entrenched patterns. The forest path is wide and well trodden. A new path will not emerge without repeated use.

Another domain where plasticity becomes strikingly concrete is rehabilitation. In 2011, researchers at the University of Zurich observed measurable cortical reorganisation in patients learning to use a robotic exoskeleton after spinal cord injury. The patterns of activation were not random; they followed the new sequences required for assisted movement. Yet the outcomes varied, influenced by the individual's medical history, the intensity of training, and the remaining neural pathways. Limitation and possibility intertwined. Plasticity enabled functional recovery but demanded persistent, structured practice—mirroring the experience of learning a new route to work, only under far more challenging conditions.

Attention emerges as the decisive lever. It determines which pathways are activated repeatedly enough to strengthen. Consider two people walking identical streets. One notices the building numbers, locates landmarks, and constructs a mental map. The other listens to music and pays little attention to the environment. After ten days, their neural maps of the route will differ markedly. The distinction lies not in exposure but in focus. *Attention is commitment rendered visible.*

This dynamic extends to emotional habits. If a person repeatedly focuses on perceived threats, their amygdala—a region involved in detecting potential danger—will fire more readily. Studies such as Whalen et al. (2001) demonstrated that even subliminal threat cues trigger amygdala activation within milliseconds. Over time, heightened responsiveness becomes the default. In contrast, training attention towards calming sensory cues or neutral stimuli engages prefrontal regions that modulate reactivity. The pattern is the same: repeated activation alters the balance between networks.

The motif of pathways returns here: the brain is always choosing which road to widen. This is not deterministic; it is probabilistic. A widened path does not force behaviour, but it makes certain responses more likely. This probabilistic nature explains why change can feel slippery. Even as new pathways begin to form, old ones remain available. Under fatigue or stress, the brain returns to whichever path is fastest. The behaviour is not a moral lapse; it is an efficiency calculation.

When considering spiritual or contemplative practices, the implications become more pointed. A person might begin a daily breathing exercise with enthusiasm, only to abandon it after three days of distraction. But if they understand that the mind's wandering is not failure but entrenched habit loops asserting themselves, the experience shifts. They can expect resistance. They can measure progress not by whether the mind is calm but by how often they return to the chosen focus. Each return is a rehearsal. Each rehearsal is a strengthening. The brain does not reward intensity; it rewards consistency.

Plasticity is not a philosophy of boundless potential; it is a discipline anchored in biology. It requires honesty about what has been rehearsed in the past and patience in rehearsing what one wishes to cultivate next. It rewards repetition, not sudden epiphany. It offers hope grounded in structure rather than sentiment. And its quiet motif—pathways widening with use—reminds us that even modest, consistent commitments can shift the terrain of inner life over time.

The unresolved tension it poses is simple: given that every thought, action, and focus of attention strengthens one path while weakening another, which path are you rehearsing today?

Belief, Attention, and Wiring

In April 1902, in a lecture hall at Harvard, William James told his students that "*My experience is what I agree to attend to.*" The line, delivered in Cambridge, Massachusetts, was more than philosophical flourish. James believed that attention shaped the contours of inner life, and that belief—what a person held to be true—guided attention like a magnet. His audience could not have known that over a century later, neuroscientists would track this claim down to measurable shifts in neural firing, showing how patterns of thought and habit recruit the same principle James intuited: what the mind returns to, the brain reinforces. His words still land with force because they describe something both intimate and observable. A single sentence captures it. *Attention directs wiring.*

Consider Mara, a 36-year-old project manager in Leeds, sitting at her desk on a grey Wednesday morning. She has made a small mistake in a report, nothing serious, but immediately a familiar phrase rises in her mind: *You're hopeless.* She does not say it aloud. She barely notices it. Yet the effect is physical—a tightening in the throat, a slight ache behind the sternum. Hours pass in this atmosphere of quiet self-reproach. That evening she tries a different practice suggested by a colleague: writing down one thing she handled with care that day. It takes thirty seconds. The next night she repeats it. Within two weeks she finds the old phrase appears less sharply. A gentler alternative surfaces: *It was a small error; you corrected it.* The shift is modest but real. The repeated act of noticing kindness—however small—begins to pull attention away from her entrenched script. A new path forms beside the old one.

The motif of a path is useful here. A path widens when walked often; it narrows when ignored. Beliefs and attention work together in much the same way. A belief is not a static idea stored in a mental cupboard. It lives through repeated activation. When someone believes they are inadequate, they rehearse that belief through what they notice, what they interpret, and how they speak to themselves. Each rehearsal strengthens a neural route. The belief feels more "true" not because evidence has deepened but because the circuitry has thickened. Showing the process makes it less mysterious. Naming it as reinforcement demonstrates its mechanics. Explaining it in terms of repeated firing brings biology into view. The implication is stark: beliefs are practices.

In 1976, at the University of Pennsylvania, Martin Seligman published work on learned helplessness, a phenomenon observed when animals exposed to uncontrollable stress later failed to act even when escape became possible. The findings carried an unsettling message about expectation shaping behaviour. When individuals believe their actions cannot change outcomes, they stop trying even when conditions shift. The study revealed how belief could narrow a behavioural repertoire. The visible behaviour was simple: animals that once pushed levers no longer moved. The metric—rate of escape attempts—collapsed. The motif of the path appears again: once the route of resignation is carved, other paths dim.

Belief does not only constrain; it can also expand. In 2010, at University College London, researchers conducting a longitudinal study on mindfulness training found increased activation in the anterior cingulate cortex during tasks requiring sustained focus. Participants who practised daily reflection displayed noticeable changes in attentional stability compared with controls. Here the visible behaviour was consistent return to a chosen focus. The metric was increased conflict-monitoring efficiency. The explanation: repeated acts of choosing where to attend altered network dynamics. The implication: reflection strengthens the pathways that support clarity.

Yet not all beliefs yield such structural shifts. Some remain cognitively endorsed but behaviourally weak. Someone may claim to value rest yet work through every weekend. They might say relationships matter yet avoid difficult conversations. The counter-example matters because it introduces a crucial limitation: beliefs only rewire the brain when attention and behaviour align with them consistently. A belief unaccompanied by attentional commitment lacks the neural rehearsal required for change. This does not contradict plasticity; it clarifies it. A new path appears only when walked, not when admired from a distance.

Spiritual traditions have long recognised this principle. The *Metta Sutta*, a Buddhist text originating around the 1st century BCE, offers repeated phrases of goodwill: "May all beings be safe," "May they be at ease." Practitioners recite them not to persuade themselves of a doctrine but to train attention towards benevolence. Show the repetition: a monk in Sri Lanka chanting at dawn. Name the practice: *metta bhavana*. Explain its mechanism: sustained focus on goodwill engages networks associated with empathy and emotional regulation. Implication: over weeks, the habit of attending to others' wellbeing becomes easier than attending to irritations. The path changes shape.

Attention here is not mere noticing. It is selection. It decides which signals enter working memory, which interpretations stick, and which reactions dominate. When someone dwells on tensions at work—reliving a colleague's curt remark or re-reading an email for implied criticism—they strengthen circuits linked to vigilance and threat. The visible behaviour is repeated checking. The metric is time spent ruminating. The result is a mind increasingly primed for danger. When the same person deliberately rehearses an alternative focus, perhaps pausing to acknowledge one constructive interaction from the day, the neural spotlight shifts. What fires together, as Donald Hebb noted in 1949, wires together.

A limitation emerges in cases of chronic anxiety. Even when individuals attempt to redirect attention, intrusive worries return with force. Some interpret this as evidence that beliefs cannot shift. Yet neuroscientific accounts suggest a different story: chronic anxiety involves overactivation of the amygdala and underactivation of regulatory prefrontal regions. The old path—threat focus—is wide and fast. The new path—meaning focus—is narrow and slow. Persisting with the narrower route does not erase anxiety; it builds capacity alongside it. Reconciliation lies in understanding timing: the brain's protective biases return early and often, but the slower circuits of reflection gain strength with steady rehearsal.

The motif of the path returns again in examining self-criticism. When Mara's inner voice softened after weeks of gentle reflection, the shift did not feel dramatic. It was almost background noise. But the behaviour had changed: fewer hours spent replaying mistakes and more moments of recognising competence. A researcher could, in principle, measure these shifts through reduced rumination time or heart-rate variability linked to emotional regulation. The path became walkable.

Beliefs shape perception through selective attention. A supervisor convinced that her team distrusts her will notice delayed replies and neutral expressions as evidence. If she holds a different belief—that her team is preoccupied but capable—she will interpret the same cues differently. Behaviour diverges. In the first case she may withdraw or micromanage. In the second she may offer support or clarification. Networks fire accordingly. The brain tracks the difference.

Two further examples, each anchored in place and date, illuminate this interplay. In 1998, at the University of Wisconsin–Madison, Richard Davidson's lab recorded the neural activity of Tibetan monks who had practised compassion meditation for decades. Their left prefrontal cortex, associated with positive affect and intentional action, showed unusually high activation compared with controls. The behaviour behind the finding was repeated compassionate focus. The implication: attention directed through belief can tilt emotional baseline. Years later, in 2015, a study in Lyon, France, found that novices who trained in similar practices for just eight weeks displayed enhanced activity in regions linked to perspective-taking. The behaviour was small: daily ten-minute sessions. The implication: even brief yet consistent attention can modify circuitry.

A counterpoint comes from cases where belief shifts without corresponding neural change. In certain behavioural interventions, participants report feeling more hopeful yet continue reacting with the same patterns under stress. Critics argue this reveals the limits of belief-based change. But closer examination shows that without repeated attentional practice, belief alone lacks the biological rehearsal needed for rewiring. The path is conceptual, not enacted. Reconciliation requires distinguishing cognitive endorsement from embodied training.

The path motif helps unify these threads. A belief is the direction. Attention is the stepping. Wiring is the ground beneath. When direction and stepping align, the ground shifts. When they diverge, the ground remains unchanged.

What does this mean for someone like Mara? It means her emerging compassionate voice is not a trick of optimism but the result of committed attention. Her visible behaviour—pausing before writing her nightly reflection—becomes the rehearsal that alters the ease with which compassion arises. Metrics could track the shift: fewer self-critical entries, more balanced interpretations, lower physiological stress responses. The implication is hopeful but disciplined: what feels natural tomorrow depends on what is rehearsed today.

The unresolved tension is this: given that attention reinforces whichever belief it serves, which belief will you allow your mind to practise tonight?

From Survival Mode to Meaning Mode

On 24 October 1957, in Moscow, neurophysiologist Evgeny Sokolov presented findings that startled his colleagues. He had been measuring the orienting response—the brain's automatic shift toward potential threat—using simple auditory tones. What he noticed was stark: within milliseconds, the body committed its full attention to any stimulus it deemed significant. Heart rate dipped, pupils widened, and the cortex reallocated resources. The phenomenon, later termed the *orienting reflex*, confirmed something long suspected but never quantified so precisely: the human nervous system prioritises potential danger with breathtaking speed. One five-word truth captures the pattern. *Threat commands the spotlight instantly.*

The relevance of Sokolov's demonstration becomes clear in an ordinary office. Imagine a meeting room in Manchester, 9:15 a.m. A team is reviewing quarterly figures. Amid the shuffle of papers and small talk, a senior manager glances sharply at Daniel, a marketing lead in his early forties. The manager's tone cuts: "Why wasn't this addressed earlier?" The room falls into momentary silence. Daniel feels heat rise in his chest. His jaw sets. His hearing narrows to the cadence of his own pulse. He wants to defend himself quickly, loudly, decisively. The behaviour is visible: hands tighten around a pen, shoulders lift, breathing shortens. From the outside, it appears reactive. From the inside, it is automatic. His brain has triggered the same circuitry Sokolov measured decades earlier—a system built for survival, not nuance.

The contrast between *survival mode* and *meaning mode* begins here, in these first visceral seconds. Survival mode is fast, narrow, and binary.

Meaning mode is slower, wider, and exploratory. The motif that threads through this subchapter—*the narrowing beam*—helps make sense of the shift. Threat shrinks the mental beam to a single, glaring point. Reflection broadens it. The challenge of modern emotional life is learning when to trust the beam and when to widen it deliberately.

Show the mechanism at work. Name its components. Explain their interaction. Then follow the implications.

When Daniel hears the critical remark, the amygdala fires first. This almond-shaped structure, long studied at institutions such as Yale and MIT, detects social threat with the same urgency it once reserved for predators. The process is measurable: within 70–100 milliseconds, the amygdala signals downstream regions to mobilise. Cortisol and adrenaline rise. Prefrontal regions responsible for perspective-taking and long-range reasoning reduce activity. The narrowing beam locks on. The implication is immediate: Daniel loses access to the very cognitive tools that would allow him to answer calmly. His brain prepares him to win or withdraw, not to think.

Examples from the historical record show this dual system clearly. In 1983, at the University of California, Joseph LeDoux conducted experiments mapping the "low road" of emotional response—fast, crude, survival-directed—and the "high road"—slower, more analytical. Rats exposed to sudden threats responded before their cortex had even processed the sound. That same architecture exists in humans. The low road tightens attention, primes the muscles, and favours speed over accuracy. The high road allows context, interpretation, and restraint. Their competition defines much of everyday conflict.

A later case from 2016 at the University of Oxford demonstrates the flip-side. When participants were guided into reflective thought—by asking them to consider someone else's viewpoint during a disagreement—functional MRI scans showed heightened activation in the medial prefrontal cortex and the temporoparietal junction, areas linked to empathy and narrative integration. The behaviour was visible too: participants paused more often, asked clarifying questions, and softened their tone. The beam widened. The implication was promising: reflective engagement can recruit networks powerful enough to counteract the narrowing force of threat.

Now return to Daniel. The meeting continues. His instinct is to retort. But in the split second before he speaks, another thought appears: *Wait.* The pause is barely a breath, but it alters the arc of the moment. The behaviour shifts. He exhales, loosens his grip on the pen, and says, "Let me check the timeline—I may have missed something." The sentence is measured, not defensive. It buys clarity. It steadies the room. His colleagues nod, the manager's tone cools, and the meeting moves on. A small triumph. Yet the deeper significance lies not in diplomacy but in wiring. Daniel has managed to access meaning mode while his physiology still hums with threat.

Show the phenomenon. Name the network. Explain the shift. Follow the implication.

Meaning mode draws on what neuroscientists call the *default mode network* (DMN) and the *frontoparietal control network* (FPCN). These systems support reflection, autobiographical thinking, moral evaluation, and mental time travel—the capacity to imagine outcomes beyond the present impulse. When the DMN and FPCN coordinate, a person can hold multiple perspectives simultaneously. They can remember past patterns, anticipate consequences, and temper reactions. Their beam broadens. Activity here is slower by design. While survival mode values seconds, meaning mode values coherence.

This is why many religious and philosophical traditions emphasised pauses, breaths, or brief invocations before speaking. In the Rule of St Benedict (c. 530 CE), monks were instructed to "listen with the ear of the heart." The phrase may sound poetic, but its behavioural component is concrete: wait, notice, respond from perspective rather than impulse. Seen through a modern lens, the instruction functions as a neural cue—an invitation to allow the high-road networks a moment to catch up.

Yet the two modes are not symmetrical in power. Survival mode has evolutionary precedence. It acts fast because it once needed to.

Meaning mode has intellectual and emotional depth but requires conditions—oxygen, time, frontal engagement—that threat disrupts. A credible counter-example surfaces here: individuals under intense stress, such as first responders or soldiers, often rely on habit rather than reflection. Their training emphasises drills and protocols precisely because the brain's reflective systems are compromised during acute threat. Far from undermining the principle of meaning mode, this demonstrates its boundary. Under extreme load, survival mode dominates. Reconciliation lies in acknowledging context: meaning mode thrives in moderate stress, practice, and relational safety, not in crisis.

The narrowing beam motif helps track how attention shifts in ordinary conflict. When Daniel first heard the criticism, his beam fixed on perceived danger: *I'm being blamed.* The phrasing of his inner thought matters; it is a behavioural marker of cognitive constriction. When he paused, he loosened the beam. His next question—*What actually happened?*—engaged networks that broaden perception. The choice of question is visible, measurable. It can be counted in meetings or heard in transcripts. The widening of the beam is not mystical; it is a behaviour.

Two further examples illuminate the competition between these networks.

In 2004, neuroscientist Tania Singer at the University of Zurich showed participants images of people receiving mild pain stimuli. Those who were instructed to observe analytically activated regions consistent with perspective-taking. Those who were simply exposed without instruction activated empathic distress circuits more strongly. Attention shaped the beam. It either contracted around discomfort or widened towards understanding. Behaviour changed accordingly; observers in the reflective condition offered more measured responses afterwards.

In 2018 at Stanford, researchers studying conflict conversations found that participants who framed disagreements using "What might I be missing?" rather than "How do I defend my point?" showed increased tolerance for ambiguity and reduced physiological stress markers. The visible behaviour was subtle: slower speech, fewer interruptions, more exploratory language. The metric—heart-rate variability—improved. The implication is straightforward: reflective questions recruit meaning mode.

Yet limitations remain. Not everyone can switch modes reliably. Individuals with post-traumatic stress or chronic hypervigilance experience persistent amygdala hyperactivation. It is not laziness or unwillingness; it is physiology. Their beam narrows rapidly and stubbornly. Does this contradict the model? No. It clarifies that survival mode's dominance varies by history, not by virtue. Reconciliation requires nuance: meaning mode is available, but its access demands gentler conditions, more repetition, and often professional support. The model holds; its thresholds differ.

The motif of the narrowing beam appears again when examining social threat. Humans depend on belonging. A critical glance in a meeting can feel existential not because the stakes are objectively high, but because exclusion once meant vulnerability. This legacy shapes behaviour. People speak more quickly, raise their voices, or shut down entirely when the beam narrows. Observers misinterpret these reactions as personality traits rather than momentary neural states. This misreading matters. It influences feedback, leadership decisions, and relational dynamics.

Conversely, the widening of the beam can be observed in everyday acts: a manager leaning back in his chair during a disagreement; a teacher pausing before responding to a challenging question; a friend asking "Say more" instead of rebutting. These are behaviours that mark meaning mode. They can be counted. They can be trained. They leave neural traces.

Returning one final time to Daniel, consider what happened after the meeting. At lunch, a colleague commended him for handling the moment with composure. Daniel admitted the remark had stung, but he had "caught himself." That catching is the crux. It is the hinge between modes. A neuroscientist could, in principle, measure the microsecond delay between amygdala firing and prefrontal regulation, but from Daniel's perspective the experience is simple: a breath, a shift, a slight widening of the internal beam. His behaviour altered the wiring that will shape his next meeting.

Sokolov's reflex still operates. The amygdala still reacts. The narrowing beam still appears. But meaning mode waits nearby, accessible through moments of deliberate attention, small acts of perspective, and the willingness to inhabit a slower circuit. The two systems coexist. Their balance defines the texture of daily life.

The unresolved question is direct: when the next critical glance narrow your beam, which mode will you choose to rehearse?

Why Spiritual Practice Needs the Brain

In February 1890, in Leipzig, Wilhelm Wundt recorded an observation that puzzled his students. During a simple attention task, participants reported moments of "inner steadiness" when they focused on a single breath, even though their hearts were racing from the apparatus used to measure reaction time. Wundt noted that these flickers of calm coincided with measurable shifts in cortical activity. The paradox was striking: a subjective experience long described in religious texts as a movement of the "heart" could be detected in the electrical rhythms of the brain. For Wundt, the implication was not to reduce the soul to circuitry but to recognise that inner life had a bodily foundation. A sentence quietly threaded through his notes captures the insight. *The invisible rests on the physical.*

Spiritual traditions have long relied on metaphors of heart, soul, and spirit to describe the terrain of transformation. These metaphors carry weight precisely because they gesture toward aspects of human life that resist quantification—longing, purpose, humility, awe. But when these same traditions prescribe concrete practices—breathing, chanting, confession, silence, repetition—they are not merely offering poetry. They are working with the machinery of attention, memory, and habit. And that machinery has a home. It is neural tissue, organised through reinforcement and shaped by use.

Show this connection. Name its mechanisms. Explain how it deepens practice. Follow the implications.

Consider Elena, a solicitor in Bristol balancing heavy caseloads with a restless mind. She begins a basic breathing practice after hearing a colleague praise its effects. The practice is simple: sit, inhale, exhale, count four breaths, then repeat. She tries it for three mornings. Each time, within seconds, her mind leaps to unfinished emails, potential mistakes, and the day's calendar. Her behaviour is predictable: fidget, sigh, check the clock. On the fourth morning she feels foolish and wants to stop. Yet she remembers hearing that habits operate in loops. She reminds herself: *cue, routine, reward.* Her cue is sitting down. The routine is breath-counting. The reward is not calm but completion. This tiny shift—knowing that she is training a loop, not chasing a feeling—keeps her on the cushion for two more minutes. Two minutes are enough. Something begins to hold.

The mechanism deserves clarity. The term *habit loop* entered psychology through research by B. F. Skinner in the mid-twentieth century, later refined through neurological studies at MIT in the early 2000s. In 2005, Ann Graybiel's team identified distinct patterns of neural firing in the basal ganglia that marked the beginning and end of habitual sequences. A behaviour repeated consistently became encoded as a single chunk. The visible sign was efficiency: rats navigated mazes faster; humans tied shoelaces without conscious thought. The explanation was structural: neurons fired in compressed bursts, signalling a transition from deliberate action to automaticity. The implication is vital for spiritual practice. A routine repeated regularly—sitting to breathe, standing to pray, pausing before speaking—eventually moves from effortful to natural. The brain begins to carry the weight.

Yet spiritual literature predates these discoveries by centuries. In the *Dhammapada* (circa 3rd century BCE), practitioners are urged to "guard the mind" through repeated attention to breath and intention. The behaviour was precise: monks in ancient Sri Lanka watched the rise and fall of the abdomen for hours. The metric, though unspoken, was consistency. The explanation, viewed through a contemporary lens, is neuroplasticity. The implication is continuity: ancient methods anticipated modern findings about repeated focus shaping neural pathways. The metaphor of "guarding the heart" made sense because the mind and body were inseparable.

A second historical example shows the same pattern. In 1678, John Bunyan published *The Pilgrim's Progress* in London, describing the moral transformation of his protagonist through repeated moments of repentance and recommitment. The story is allegorical, but the underlying structure is behavioural. Christian communities in seventeenth-century England practised daily examination—cataloguing thoughts, actions, and intentions. The behaviour was visible: writing reflections, kneeling at night, confessing missteps. The implicit mechanism aligns with what neuroscientists today call error monitoring and metacognitive awareness. The implication again is clear. Spiritual traditions have always paired reflection with repetition because the brain responds to repeated checks of intention and action by strengthening the circuits that support them.

Yet there is a limitation. Not all spiritual practices lead to beneficial rewiring. Repetition alone does not guarantee growth. A counter-example surfaces in cases of scrupulosity, a condition documented in monastic writings from medieval Europe. In 1215, at the Fourth Lateran Council in Rome, clergy expressed concern that excessive confession produced cycles of guilt rather than liberation. Behaviourally, individuals confessed dozens of times a day. Metrics, though crude, appeared in records noting hours spent in penitence. The implication was troubling: repetition can reinforce anxiety if the content of attention is fear. This does not undermine the connection between practice and brain change; it emphasises the need for wise content. The motif that threads through this subchapter—the difference between *heavy loops* and *light loops*—helps clarify. Heavy loops reinforce shame. Light loops reinforce meaning.

Returning to Elena deepens the theme. After a fortnight of brief, structured breathing, she notices something unexpected. In a meeting where a partner questions her analysis, her breath tightens—but she catches it. She inhales once, slowly, before replying. The behaviour is small: two seconds of pause. The metric: one breath. Yet that breath recruits the prefrontal circuits strengthened during her morning practice. The beam of attention widens. She replies without defensiveness. This is not serenity in the abstract; it is a trained neural shift under pressure.

Show the process. Name the network. Explain the function. Follow the implication.

The medial prefrontal cortex (mPFC), often activated during reflective practices, connects to regions governing emotional regulation. When Elena counted breaths, she repeatedly activated this network. When confronted in the meeting, the mPFC had enough strength to counter the amygdala's immediate alarm. The implication is fundamental: spiritual practices that emphasise attention and emotional steadiness are not chasing transcendence; they are training neural regulators.

To see this dynamic from a different angle, consider a 2003 study at the University of Wisconsin–Madison by Antoine Lutz and colleagues. They measured gamma synchrony in long-term meditators—monks trained in Tibetan Buddhist traditions. Behaviourally, these monks had practised compassion and awareness for tens of thousands of hours. The metric, gamma synchrony, indicated large-scale neural integration. The explanation was straightforward: years of repeated contemplative focus had tuned the brain's rhythms. The implication is not that hours equate to holiness, but that practice changes structure. Heavy loops give way to light loops.

A second modern example reinforces the connection. In 2014, at Stanford, researchers found that participants who practised simple loving-kindness phrases for eight weeks showed increased activation in regions linked to social cognition when viewing distressed faces. Behaviour: silent recitation of phrases such as "May you be safe." Metric: change in neural activation. Explanation: repeated attention to goodwill primed the brain for empathic perception. Implication: spiritual intentions become perceptual habits.

Yet limitations still matter. Some individuals attempt contemplative practice while experiencing acute trauma responses. Their nervous systems may be too sensitised for practices that require stillness. In such cases, stillness can amplify distress. Does this contradict the premise that spiritual practice needs the brain? No. It affirms it. Understanding the brain's thresholds guides the type, duration, and intensity of practice. A person in acute hypervigilance may need movement-based grounding before breath-counting becomes safe. Knowledge of the body's mechanisms makes practice more humane.

This brings us to a recurring motif: the loop. Every spiritual practice contains a loop—cue, routine, reward. The cue might be dawn light on a window, the sound of a bell, or the moment before a meal. The routine might be breath-counting, chanting, reading a verse, or sitting in silence. The reward is not always emotional uplift. Sometimes it is a sense of completion, coherence, or alignment with intention. The brain registers the loop. The loop reinforces the wiring.

But loops fail when expectations are unrealistic. Elena initially believed breathing practice should produce calm. It didn't. Calm was not the early reward; completion was. Knowing this changed her behaviour. She committed to counting ten breaths. That was the measurable target. Her loop was small. Achievable. Light. The implication ripples outward: spiritual practice becomes sustainable when built on accurate models of how the brain adapts.

Consider again the historical anchor. When Benedictine monks paused seven times a day to pray, as instructed in the *Rule of St Benedict* (c. 530 CE), the behaviour was meticulously structured. The cues were bells. The routines were psalms. The reward was communal coherence and spiritual orientation. They were training loops. They were tuning attention. Without modern terminology, they were shaping their neural responses to daily stress by interspersing their routines with breath, chant, and silence. Their loops were light and regular. Their effects were cumulative.

And yet, despite this deep history, many contemporary practitioners still approach spiritual exercises as though they operate through mystery rather than mechanism. When a practice feels dry, they assume personal failure. When distraction surges, they assume lack of aptitude. When emotions intensify rather than quieten, they assume something is wrong. The misunderstanding lies not in the practice but in the expectations surrounding it. Knowing how the brain works reframes the task. Distraction is not failure; it is the return of heavy loops. Emotion is not error; it is unprocessed information becoming visible. Stillness is not passivity; it is neural retraining.

The motif of heavy and light loops returns here. Heavy loops are reinforced by stress, habit, and past experience. They activate automatically. Light loops must be rehearsed. The task of spiritual practice is to widen the light loops until they carry more weight. It is slow work. It is steady work. It is embodied work.

Which brings us to the central claim: spiritual practice needs the brain because spiritual change is implemented through neural change. This does not diminish the language of heart or soul. It grounds it. The heart softens when the amygdala quietens. The soul expands when the prefrontal cortex has the strength to hold multiple perspectives. The spirit deepens when the networks supporting empathy and meaning grow more coherent. These statements remain metaphorical in the poetic sense, but concrete in the neural sense. They do not reduce human experience; they explain its mechanisms.

A tension remains. If every practice becomes a loop, and every loop reshapes the brain, how does one choose which loops to build? Which routines deserve rehearsal? Which cues should anchor the day? Which rewards reinforce meaning rather than mere efficiency? The next step of the journey depends on answering a simple, disquieting question: *Which loop will you train tomorrow morning?*

Chapter 2
Wounds in the Wiring: Trauma, Habit, and the Soul

On certain mornings, before she is fully awake, Leah experiences a familiar tightening in her chest. The day has not yet begun, no conversation has taken a wrong turn, no conflict has appeared on the horizon. Yet something in her braces for it. She opens her messages expecting evidence of disappointment; she interprets a delayed reply as confirmation that she has annoyed someone; she rehearses, silently and without intention, the posture of a person already preparing to be dismissed. Nothing catastrophic ever happens, yet her body acts as though it has. By mid-morning she finds herself quieter than she meant to be, more cautious, slightly withdrawn, scanning for the moment she imagines will prove her anxieties right. The tragedy is not that people reject her. The tragedy is that her nervous system is so used to anticipating rejection that it receives the world in its image.

Most wounds that shape a life are subtle. Loud traumas do exist, of course, and they deserve sober attention. But for many people, the marks that matter were formed in quieter rooms: a parent who snapped unpredictably, a friend who knew how to wound with timing rather than force, a teacher who made warmth conditional, a partner whose affection depended on compliance. Long before the brain acquires adult vocabulary—attachment, triggers, patterns—it acquires adult reflexes. It learns where to contract and where to numb, when to brace and when to withdraw. Long after the original moments pass, those reflexes remain, woven into the circuitry that shapes expectations and choices. The body remembers not with nostalgia but with prediction.

This chapter enters the territory where psychology, neuroscience, and spirituality meet: the place where pain becomes pattern, and pattern becomes identity. It does so not to reopen wounds but to understand their mechanics, because understanding transforms shame into coherence and helplessness into capacity. If the previous chapter explored how the brain longs for more, this one confronts why it struggles to believe change is possible at all. A nervous system trained in vigilance does not trust ease. A mind steeped in self-criticism does not trust kindness. A body accustomed to walking on emotional eggshells does not trust calm. What we call "personality" often begins as defence.

Emotional pain leaves traces in the brain not through poetry but through practice. When someone repeatedly experiences uncertainty or threat—whether through conflict, inconsistency, or subtle forms of dismissal—specific neural networks strengthen. Circuits involved in scanning for danger fire more quickly. Networks linked to social interpretation shift towards suspicion or hyper-alertness. Over time, these circuits do not simply respond to the world; they filter it. The motif that threads through this chapter—the groove—captures the effect. A groove in a record guides the needle. A groove in the mind guides attention. Under stress, we fall back into grooves not because we choose to but because they are familiar, efficient, and deeply rehearsed.

The grooves of habit form in ordinary life as well. A single pattern of irritation in a family—perhaps a parent who interrupts, or a sibling who deflects with humour, or a partner who raises an eyebrow at the wrong moment—can, over years, train a reliable emotional response. That response soon occurs outside the original context. Someone who learnt to defend themselves with sharpness as a teenager may find that same sharpness rising decades later with their own children, even when they intend patience. Someone who learnt to stay quiet to avoid conflict may find their adult voice fading the moment tension appears. These small grooves often feel personal, even fated, but they are patterns formed by repetition. They echo the spiritual language of bondage or samsara—cycles one did not choose yet continues to enact.

Shame, too, has its grooves. Of all emotional patterns, shame is among the stickiest because it recruits networks designed for social survival. A person who made one significant mistake years earlier may still find themselves replaying the moment in high definition, their stomach tightening as though the event is happening again. The cognitive content may vary—"I should have known better," "They must think I'm foolish," "I always ruin things"—but the physiological imprint is consistent. The body curves inward. Breathing shallows. Attention narrows to the memory as though inspecting a wound that refuses to close. Certain forms of religious upbringing, especially those heavy with moral fear rather than moral formation, can inadvertently deepen these grooves. When guilt is paired with threat, the brain memorises the pairing. It learns to meet error not with repair but with self-punishment.

Yet even the deepest grooves can be mapped, and mapping them is often the first act of liberation. Honest mapping does not require excavation of every childhood moment or a forensic audit of one's past. It begins with noticing: the pattern that appears in conflict, the story that surfaces during stress, the bodily posture that accompanies disappointment. A person might sit with a notebook one evening and write a single line—"When I don't receive an immediate reply, I feel dismissed"—and then trace what unfolds next. They might notice the tightening of their jaw, the urge to withdraw, the flood of old interpretations. Seeing the sequence clearly is not a small thing. It breaks the illusion that the reaction "just happens." It reveals the groove.

Once seen, grooves begin to loosen. Not immediately, and not through force, but through the quiet recognition that patterns are not prophecies. The person who always anticipates rejection begins to notice that sometimes people are simply busy. The person who always reacts with anger realises the reaction flares fastest when they feel unheard, not when they feel truly wronged. The person who replays the old mistake discovers that the memory appears most readily when they are tired, not when they are clear. This kind of clarity does not erase wounds, but it grants the dignity of perspective.

The significance of this chapter lies in its refusal to collapse human pain into mere biology while also refusing to romanticise it. Trauma, whether grand or subtle, reshapes the brain. Habit repeats the shaping. Shame deepens the impression. Spiritual life often begins with the longing to break free from these cycles, yet without understanding their mechanics, people mistake grooves for identity. They feel "stuck," "broken," or "spiritually dry" not because they lack wisdom but because their wiring has been trained by experience rather than intention.

At the same time, the soul—understood here as the dimension of personhood concerned with longing, significance, and deep emotional truth—does not stand apart from these processes. It expresses itself through them. The ache one feels when a pattern repeats is itself a spiritual signal: a recognition that the groove does not honour the life one wishes to live. The frustration one feels after snapping at a loved one, or withdrawing too quickly, or replaying the same shame memory, is not simply self-reproach. It is a longing for coherence. It is the spirit nudging the mind towards change.

The path ahead in this chapter is rigorous but hopeful. It will examine how pain lays foundations, how habits reinforce them, how shame cements them, and how honest mapping begins to release them. It will not offer platitudes; it will not suggest that naming a wound is enough to heal it. But it will insist that understanding the grooves—where they came from, how they function, and why they persist—grants a kind of agency that spiritual clichés cannot provide.

In the wider context of this book, this chapter plays a crucial role. Before one can cultivate compassion, or gratitude, or presence, one must understand the patterns that compete with them. Before one can sustain spiritual practice, one must recognise why the mind drifts toward old grooves under pressure. Before one can rewire towards meaning, one must understand how wires were laid in the first place.

There is, however, a deeper tension that runs beneath all of this. If the grooves of pain shape perception, how does one trust new interpretations? If habits feel like personality, how does one discern what is authentic? If shame mimics conscience, how does one tell the difference? These questions hover at the edges of transformation. They signal the threshold between seeing a pattern and stepping beyond it.

The pages that follow will not answer them in a single stroke. Instead, they will invite a slow, honest examination of one's own wiring—not as self-indulgence, but as preparation for change. They will show how wounds can be acknowledged without being enshrined, how habits can be observed without being obeyed, and how the soul can reclaim authority over the patterns that once dictated its movements.

The grooves remain. The question is whether they remain in control.

How Pain Leaves Traces

In July 1907, at the Salpêtrière Hospital in Paris, Pierre Janet documented a case that unsettled many of his contemporaries. A woman named Marie, who had endured years of marital volatility, exhibited an unmistakable reflex whenever he raised his voice in the slightest: her shoulders tensed, her gaze dropped, and her breathing shortened. Janet recorded that the reaction occurred even when the content of his words was neutral. The behaviour was automatic. The trigger was tone alone. He concluded that her nervous system had "memorised" the threat long after she had consciously left it behind. A short sentence from his notebook captures the intuition. *The past repeats itself in the body.*

The trace of pain rarely announces itself with spectacle. More often it surfaces quietly, in the small ways a person moves through a room or reads a silence. Consider Leah, a capable analyst in London, who hesitates before entering a meeting not because of the agenda but because she fears she will be dismissed. She checks her phone repeatedly for messages she expects will contain disappointment. She reads a neutral email twice, searching for an implied slight. Her visible behaviour—drawing back in conversation, offering opinions with a pre-emptive apology—reveals a posture shaped not by the present but by old experiences of unpredictability. These behaviours are not melodramatic. They are patterned. They are grooves.

The motif of the groove matters here. A groove deepens with repeated movement. Neural circuits sculpt themselves in a similar fashion. When the brain encounters difficult experiences—conflict, inconsistency, humiliation, exclusion—it recruits threat pathways to protect the organism. Show the reaction: the body tightens, scanning intensifies, the breath shortens. Name the structures: the amygdala, the insula, the anterior cingulate cortex. Explain the process: repeated activation strengthens the connections among these regions, making vigilance the mind's default. Follow the implication: what began as a protective reflex can become a way of seeing.

One can track this in measurable phenomena. In 1998, Bessel van der Kolk at Massachusetts General Hospital used neuroimaging to observe how trauma survivors responded to cues associated with their experiences. Their brains lit up in regions linked to threat even when the cues were symbolic. Participants showed visible behaviours—hands clenched, voices tightened—while recalling events from years earlier. The implication was clear: pain does not remain in memory alone; it alters the circuitry of anticipation.

A second named example, drawn from 2012 research at the University of Zürich, adds nuance. Andrea Meyer and colleagues examined adults with histories of relational instability. When asked to anticipate rejection during a controlled laboratory task, participants displayed heightened activity in the dorsal anterior cingulate cortex—a region associated with social pain. The behaviour mirrored this: longer pauses before responding, reduced eye contact, more frequent self-correction. The past shaped not only what participants feared but how they behaved while fearing it.

Yet there are limits. Not every person who experiences emotional difficulty develops entrenched patterns. One credible counter-example comes from the longitudinal Dunedin Study in New Zealand. Though some participants with early adversity developed heightened vigilance, others displayed remarkable resilience, forming balanced expectations in adulthood despite similar stressors. This variation does not undermine the principle of neural shaping; it introduces complexity. Genetic differences, supportive relationships, and timing of stressors all modulate susceptibility. Reconciliation lies in understanding that while pain often leaves traces, its depth and persistence depend on context.

Still, the grooves form more often than we admit. And they form not only through dramatic harms but through everyday micro-experiences—coldness, comparison, correction, inconsistency—that accumulate into expectation. Show it in Leah's weekly routine. She arrives early to avoid being judged for lateness. She rephrases sentences twice before speaking. When a colleague frowns at their laptop, she assumes it is directed at her. The brain is not calculating logically; it is predicting based on learned cues. The groove directs her attention toward possible rejection.

Name the mechanism behind this prediction error. Cognitive neuroscientists refer to it as a "prior"—an expectation encoded through experience. Explain how it forms: repeated exposure to dismissal teaches the brain that exclusion is likely, so it biases perception. Visible implication: when someone pauses before responding, Leah hears criticism rather than thoughtfulness.

Historical accounts show this pattern long before neuroimaging could capture it. In 5th-century BCE China, Confucius described a pupil who "held his heart as though trouble were ahead." The phrase, preserved in the *Analects*, described a bodily posture that modern psychologists would recognise instantly—a vigilant tilt toward anticipated harm. Though the language differed, the mechanism mapped neatly: pain shapes readiness.

Numbness, a related trace, follows a different groove. Instead of hyper-alertness, the nervous system withdraws. The behaviour is muted: slow speech, reduced facial expression, a slight delay in responding. In 2015, a study at King's College London found that individuals with prolonged emotional suppression showed decreased activation in the anterior insula—an area linked to interoception. Their bodies had learned not to feel, because feeling once signalled danger. The implication is significant. Numbness is not apathy; it is adaptation.

Reactivity—another trace—forms when emotional circuits fire with minimal provocation. A child who grows up trying to manage parental tension may learn to intervene quickly, loudly, automatically. As an adult, that same person may find irritation rising before comprehension catches up. Behavioural markers include raised voice, faster speech, and abrupt gestures. The motif of the groove returns: when reactivity is rehearsed, it becomes quick, smooth, efficient.

But pain's traces do not remain private. They shape relationships. Leah withdraws pre-emptively, which her friends interpret as distance. A colleague trained in conflict responds defensively to mild queries. A partner accustomed to soothing others becomes drained by their own vigilance. Each participant's grooves interact with the others', forming patterns at the level of families, teams, and communities.

The implication expands. If the groove of vigilance expects rejection, it will find it—or interpret neutrality as equivalent. If the groove of numbness expects overwhelm, it will mute sensation until the world feels flat. If the groove of reactivity expects threat, it will sense danger even in gentle correction. Behaviour becomes expectation enacted.

Yet a limitation must be acknowledged. Not all vigilance is maladaptive. In certain contexts—clinical wards, high-conflict workplaces, environments with real risk—heightened alertness can be protective. The behaviour may appear tense, but the metric of risk reduction can justify it. Reconciliation requires distinguishing between vigilance that matches the environment and vigilance imported from an old landscape into a new one. Leah's workplace does not mirror her family home, but her body cannot yet tell the difference.

A quiet motif weaves through these patterns: *the body leans.* Leah's body leans away before anyone has approached. Marie's shoulders lean inward before anyone has shouted. The policeman whose reactivity developed from years of high-stress encounters leans forward before anyone has acted. Leaning—literal or figurative—reveals the groove.

Two final examples reinforce the interplay between experience and wiring. In 2007, Naomi Eisenberger at UCLA demonstrated that social exclusion activates the same neural networks as physical pain. Behaviourally, participants who believed they were left out of a digital ball-tossing game showed slumped posture and reduced speech. Metric: increased activation in the dorsal anterior cingulate cortex. Implication: everyday hurts have biological weight.

In 2019, a study at the University of Cambridge found that adolescents subjected to chronic criticism displayed heightened amygdala response to neutral faces. The behaviour mirrored this: they interpreted neutral expressions as hostile more often than controls. The implication: expectations of harm become templates through which ambiguity is read.

These findings echo what spiritual traditions have long intuited: hurt shapes perception. It shapes posture. It shapes interpretation. It shapes what the heart thinks it sees.

Which raises the unresolved tension: if grooves form from repeated pain, how does one learn to trust new paths that feel unfamiliar, or even unsafe? And when the body leans away before the mind has spoken, what does it mean to choose a different direction?

Habit Loops and Spiritual Stuckness

In February 1898, at Johns Hopkins University in Baltimore, Henry F. Osborn demonstrated a principle that would echo far beyond the laboratory. While studying conditioned motor responses in primates, he observed that, once an action had been repeated enough times, the animal performed it even when the original cue was removed. One sequence—light, lever, food—eventually collapsed into a single automatic gesture. Osborn noted that the behaviour persisted for weeks. A five-word observation captured his conclusion. *Repetition reduces choice over time.* His remark was meant for biologists, yet its reach extends deeply into human experience, especially the experience of feeling emotionally or spiritually stuck.

You can see the same mechanism unfold in an ordinary household. Consider David, standing at his kitchen counter in Sheffield, a cup of tea cooling beside him. His teenage son makes a casual comment—"You never listen anyway"—uttered with more frustration than intent. David's jaw tightens. A familiar heat rises. He responds sharply. His voice lifts half a pitch. His shoulders tense. Within seconds, the room carries the weight of another argument neither of them meant to start. Afterwards, David wonders, *Why did I react like that again?* But the loop is already running. The cue was the tone. The routine was irritation. The reward—if it can be called that—was the fleeting sense of regaining control. Behaviour, circuitry, and emotion folded into one groove.

The motif of the groove reappears throughout this subchapter, because grooves illustrate how habit and identity can become confused. A groove feels like a fact. A loop feels like a personality trait. With enough rehearsal, the brain treats the pattern as default, even destiny. Yet what looks like fate is often only practice.

Show this. Name it. Explain it. Follow its implications.

The habit loop—cue, routine, reward—was rigorously mapped a century after Osborn, through the work of Ann Graybiel's team at MIT in 2005. They observed "chunking": repeated behaviours compressed into neural packets that fired at the beginning and end of an action sequence. The visible behaviour was efficiency—rats sprinted through mazes they had once walked tentatively. The metric was neural firing patterns in the dorsal striatum. The explanation was structural: repetition moved behaviours from deliberate control to automatic execution. The implication for human habit is sobering. When emotional routines chunk, they become reflexes.

Different traditions intuited this long before neuroscience. In the Buddhist *Pali Canon* (circa 1st century BCE), teachers described samsara as "the wheel that turns itself." The phrase referred not only to metaphysics but to psychology: cycles of reaction that perpetuate suffering because they run automatically. A practitioner scolds a companion before thinking. A parent repeats their own parents' tone. A monk returns to distraction despite intention. Functionally, these are loops: cue, routine, reward. The language of bondage in Christian monastic writings of the 4th century—"the heart bound to its vice"—captures a similar insight. Behaviour rehearsed becomes behaviour believed.

In David's case, the loop took years to form. His father had responded swiftly and harshly to perceived disrespect. The behaviour became the model. The cue was raised tone. The routine was a sharp retort. The reward—a momentary sense of strength—was small but consistent. David's adult brain still registers critique through that inherited circuitry. The groove holds.

One can measure such grooves. A 2014 study from the University of Cambridge found that adults who grew up in unpredictable or critical environments showed heightened activation in the dorsal anterior cingulate cortex when receiving ambiguous feedback. Their behaviour mirrored this: abrupt speech, defensive posture, premature interruption. The metric: increased error-alerting signals. The explanation: repeated exposure to criticism trained the brain to expect conflict. The implication is direct: old loops stealthily shape present reactions.

A second example, published in 2016 by researchers at the University of Toronto, examined couples engaged in conflict tasks. Partners with entrenched anger patterns showed faster amygdala activation in response to neutral facial expressions. Their behaviour—elevated pitch within seconds, clipped phrasing—revealed how quickly the loop ignited. The brain had chunked anger into a near-instantaneous routine.

A credible limitation complicates the picture: not all repeated behaviour becomes automatic. Some people rehearse reactions for years and still retain conscious control. Consider professionals in emergency medicine. Their work exposes them to repeated stress cues, yet many display finely regulated responses. Their behaviour—slowed speech, measured decisions—remains deliberate. Metrics such as reaction-time consistency and heart-rate variability reveal trained modulation. This does not contradict habit loops; it highlights that deliberate counter-practice can prevent chunking. Reconciliation lies in distinguishing repetition saturated with awareness from repetition driven by fear.

Still, for most people, emotional loops run themselves long before awareness intervenes. And when these loops echo spiritual themes—bondage, compulsion, samsara—the sense of stuckness can deepen. Someone may say, "I'm just an angry person," when what they mean is, "My loop ignites faster than I can catch it." Another may say, "I withdraw because I'm introverted," when what they enact is a protective routine rehearsed since adolescence. The loop feels like identity. The groove feels like truth.

This confusion becomes particularly costly in family life, where loops interact. David's sharp tone is met by his son's defensive shrug. The son's shrug becomes a cue for further irritation. The room contracts around the cycle. The motif of the groove appears again: the more the loop runs, the smoother it becomes. Without deliberate interruption, it becomes the household's emotional choreography.

Historical sources show how such loops were recognised even without neural vocabulary. In 1651, Blaise Pascal wrote in *Pensées* that humans live "pushed by habits, dragged by inclinations." His description, though framed theologically, maps cleanly onto contemporary models of compressed behavioural sequences. His implication was both moral and mechanical: one becomes what one repeatedly does.

Modern neuroscience adds specificity. When emotional reactions harden into habit, the orbitofrontal cortex (involved in evaluating outcomes) reduces its influence relative to basal ganglia circuits. Behaviour becomes less about meaning and more about momentum. The shift is observable in laboratory tasks measuring cognitive flexibility. People with entrenched loops struggle to adapt when rules change. Their reactions lag behind context. In David's case, his son's frustration in a single conversation triggers years of rehearsed authority rather than the real-time nuance needed for a new relationship.

Another limitation worth noting is cultural. Some cultures explicitly value certain loops—stoicism, deference, emotional neatness—because they maintain harmony in community. These loops can be adaptive within their context, even if they appear restrictive elsewhere. The implication is that spiritual stuckness must be interpreted within culture; a loop is not dysfunctional merely because it is automatic. It becomes problematic when it contradicts one's values or causes harm.

The motif returns in a different form: *the wheel ruts into itself.* The wheel image, present in ancient Indian texts describing cyclic existence, helps visualise how habit loops create a sense of enclosure. When the wheel turns, it deepens its own path. The longer it spins, the more difficult it becomes to shift direction. People speak of "being in a rut" because the metaphor is literal: grooves resist deviation.

The spiritual cost arises when a person mistakes the rut for destiny. They feel trapped not by doctrine but by physiology. They interpret their own reactivity as moral failure rather than a predictable neural sequence. They read their withdrawal as spiritual dryness rather than protective habit. They judge their impatience as character rather than cue. And in doing so, they reinforce the very loops from which they long to be free.

Two further examples deepen the picture. In 2003, researchers at Duke University found that nearly 40 per cent of daily actions are performed out of habit, not decision. The metric—behavioural sampling across contexts—revealed that the brain prefers efficiency over reflection. Implication: if spiritual practice aims to transform character, it must contend with the fact that much of character is automatic.

In 2018, a team at the University of Oxford examining habitual rumination noted that people consumed with self-critical thoughts activated neural loops associated with perseverative thinking in the subgenual cingulate cortex. Their behaviour—replaying the same narrative repeatedly—aligned with spiritual descriptions of bondage to thought. The implication: without intervention, mental loops mirror behavioural ones.

A counter-example complicates the narrative again. Some repeated acts—thank-you notes, small rituals, evening walks—do not produce stuckness but freedom. Their loop is gentle. Their reward aligns with meaning. The groove they carve is spacious, not constricting. This does not negate habit loops; it shows that loops differ in content and consequence. Reconciliation lies in learning to tell which grooves shrink the self and which expand it.

In David's kitchen, the loop ignited in seconds. But the very fact that he noticed the repetition afterwards—*I did it again*—indicates a thin seam of freedom. Awareness does not erase the groove, but it marks its edge. And once the edge is visible, a person can begin to ask the questions that break its spell.

Which brings the unresolved tension into focus. If loops feel like identity and grooves feel like fate, how does one begin to distinguish the self from the circuitry? And when the wheel ruts so deeply into its path, what gives someone the courage to steer in a different direction?

Shame, Guilt, and the Inner Critic

In April 1954, at University College London, the neurologist Sir John Eccles presented findings that startled an audience accustomed to thinking of morality as the domain of philosophy rather than physiology. While studying rapid shifts in self-evaluative thought, Eccles observed that a single memory of failure—spoken aloud by a participant named Margaret—triggered not only emotional discomfort but a measurable surge of activity in regions of the brain associated with self-referential judgment. The cortex fired in tight, repetitive bursts. Her breathing quickened. Her gaze fell to the floor. She whispered, "I never get things right." The behaviour was visible. The neural response was precise. Eccles concluded that moral emotions such as guilt did not simply colour experience; they carved patterns. His remark in the conference transcript reads almost as a warning. *Repetition can make the harshest voice feel like home.*

One sees this principle unfold quietly every day. Take Ravi, forty-two, living in Birmingham, who still replays a mistake he made three years ago during a presentation. He stumbled on a slide, misquoted a number by a wide margin, and noticed his manager raise an eyebrow. The audience had moved on within minutes, but Ravi did not. The memory returns whenever he feels even slightly off-balance. It arrives uninvited, vivid, charged. His behaviour shifts immediately: shoulders sink, speech softens, dinner plans are cancelled, and he says "Sorry" before he has done anything wrong. The shame loop ignites with the efficiency of muscle memory. The motif that threads through this subchapter—the echo—captures it. Shame echoes longer than the event that produced it.

Show the pattern. Name its circuitry. Explain the mechanics. Follow the implication.

Shame is not merely an emotion; it is a neurological choreography involving the medial prefrontal cortex (mPFC), the posterior cingulate cortex, and the anterior insula—regions that evaluate self, monitor error, and register social threat. When a shame memory activates, these regions fire together in a synchronised loop. The visible behaviour is withdrawal: eyes lower, shoulders round, breathing constricts. The explanation is structural: repeated self-blame strengthens the connectivity among these regions, making harsh thoughts faster and more believable. The implication is stark. A person does not merely remember shame; their brain rehearses it.

Evidence for this dynamic is robust. In 2007, Naomi Eisenberger at UCLA demonstrated that social exclusion activates many of the same neural circuits as physical pain. Participants who believed they had been ignored in a simple digital game showed increased activity in the dorsal anterior cingulate cortex. Their behaviour mirrored distress—posture collapsed, responses faltered. The metric was neural activation; the implication was biological weight: shame is not metaphorically painful; it is literally processed as pain.

A second example, from 2016 at the University of British Columbia, examined adults prone to chronic self-criticism. When asked to recall personal failures, participants showed heightened activation in the subgenual anterior cingulate cortex—a region associated with persistent negative mood states. Behaviourally, they spoke more slowly, avoided eye contact, and corrected themselves mid-sentence even when they were already correct. The loop deepened as they spoke. Shame trained its own pathways.

Yet there is a credible limitation. Not all cultures treat guilt and shame the same way. Anthropologist Ruth Benedict's 1946 distinction between "guilt cultures" and "shame cultures"—though now debated—highlights this. In some communities, shame is social glue, moderating behaviour and reinforcing belonging. In such settings, shame can be adaptive, not corrosive. The reconciliation comes in noticing that the danger lies not in momentary shame but in chronic, internalised shame—shame that outlasts context and becomes identity.

Identity shaped by shame is a particular kind of wound. It is sticky. It lingers. It loops.

This looping is evident in Ravi's story. The initial mistake was trivial: one misquoted number. But because he had grown up in a household where errors were heavily scrutinised, the cue—a raised eyebrow—triggered a familiar routine. The routine was self-blame: *You always fail when it matters.* The reward—though damaging—was predictability. Shame gave him a script he knew. That predictability is why the loop stayed. The echo felt safer than uncertainty.

Historical texts understood this stickiness. In *The Confessions* (397 CE), Augustine described being "bound by a chain of my own forging" when recalling youthful misdeeds. The phrase captures a psychological pattern: shame becomes self-reinforcing. Behaviourally, Augustine withdrew into internal monologue; emotionally, he treated the memory as morally diagnostic rather than situational. His description aligns with modern findings: shame constructs narratives that swallow context.

Another example appears in the diaries of John Wesley during the Methodist revivals of the 1740s. Wesley recorded congregants who, after hearing fiery sermons, "laboured under heavy thoughts of unworthiness." Many reported cycles of self-reproach that lasted days. Wesley eventually softened his approach, recognising that repeated exposure to moral fear produced not transformation but paralysis. The motif of the echo appears centuries before neural imaging: the spiritual life distorted by repetitive internal assault.

A counter-example offers nuance. Within some monastic traditions—particularly Benedictine and Trappist communities—confession is framed not as self-condemnation but as a truthful encounter with one's limitations. Behaviourally, monks confess briefly, without embellishment, and return to routine. Neural studies of contemplative practitioners (e.g., Lutz et al., Wisconsin, 2003) show increased activation in regions associated with emotional regulation. Their guilt loops do not spiral. The echo is quiet. Reconciliation lies in intention: shame loops harden when paired with fear; they soften when paired with acceptance.

Shame's persistence is tied to one more mechanism: memory consolidation. Highly emotional memories are replayed during sleep, strengthening their neural footprint. In 2014, researchers at Harvard demonstrated that negative emotional events are recalled more vividly after sleep than neutral ones. The behaviour in waking life is clear: people replay embarrassing episodes with more detail than joyful ones. The implication is sobering. Shame rehearses itself even in rest.

This dynamic often begins early, shaped by family patterns or religious upbringings. In households where obedience is prized over exploration, a child may internalise the belief that mistakes threaten belonging. In certain religious environments—particularly those emphasising damnation, perfectionism, or moral surveillance—children may interpret correction as existential verdict rather than guidance. A five-word phrase becomes a lifelong groove: *You are not enough again.*

Such grooves produce a specific posture of the soul: contraction. Behaviour shows it in micro-expressions—tension around the eyes, a slight curl of the shoulders, a premature apology. Speech patterns echo it—sentences that begin with "Sorry, but…" or end abruptly to avoid perceived overreach. The motif returns: the echo. Shame repeats even when uninvited.

Two more studies clarify the issue. In 2012, at the University of Manchester, researchers observed that individuals prone to self-criticism exhibited reduced connectivity between the prefrontal cortex and the amygdala during self-referential tasks. The metric was diminished regulatory control. The behaviour was visible: difficulty interrupting negative rumination. Implication: the inner critic not only speaks harshly; it weakens neural brakes that could moderate it.

In 2019, a study at King's College London showed that people dwelling on shame memories displayed increased cortisol levels even hours later. The behaviour—restlessness, difficulty concentrating—mirrored physiological arousal. Implication: shame is not just cognitive; it is hormonal.

Yet a limitation remains. Not every act of self-correction is harmful. Some forms of guilt are moral anchors, helping societies function. Behaviour such as apologising promptly, repairing mistakes, or reflecting carefully can maintain trust. These acts do not spiral because they resolve. The echo fades. The reconciliation is crucial: guilt that leads to repair is healthy; guilt that loops becomes shame.

Returning to Ravi, what he experiences is not reflection but rumination. Reflection asks, "What happened?" Rumination insists, "It happened because you are flawed." The difference is not semantic; it is neurological. Reflection activates networks associated with problem-solving; rumination activates networks that reinforce identity-based condemnation. Shame hijacks the narrative.

This subchapter sits at a critical juncture in the book. If pain leaves traces and habits form grooves, shame supplies the glue that keeps those grooves rigid. Shame convinces a person that their patterns are not patterns but personality. It whispers that reactivity is character, that withdrawal is essence, that hesitation is identity. And yet its authority is borrowed. It is a voice rehearsed, not a truth revealed.

Which brings us to the unresolved question that opens the next phase of inquiry: when a shame echo rises, carrying the weight of years, how does one distinguish the remembered verdict from the self one is still capable of becoming?

The First Step: Honest Mapping

In March 1974, at the University of Pennsylvania, psychologist Philip Brickman recorded a pattern he found more revealing than the experiment he was running. His study involved emotional adaptation, but what caught his attention was the way participants spontaneously narrated their reactions. One woman, asked about a minor disappointment, described not only the event but the cascade of sensations that followed: heat rising in her chest, an urge to retreat, a certainty that she had "messed up again." Brickman noticed that her physiological response preceded her interpretation, yet her interpretation amplified the physiology. The sequence—trigger, bodily shift, story, behaviour—was so consistent that he wrote a note in the margin of his transcript: *Patterns repeat before they are believed.* It was the beginning of what later scholars would call "affect mapping," long before the term existed.

A similar sequence unfolds in quieter, domestic settings every day. Take Anna, thirty-eight, sitting at her dining table in Leeds late on a Tuesday night. She has just received a brief text from a close friend cancelling their lunch the next day. The message is polite. There is no implied criticism. Yet Anna feels a drop in her stomach, followed by a tightening in her jaw. A familiar thought rises—*I must have done something*—before she has even placed her phone down. By the time she walks to the kitchen for a glass of water, she has constructed a small narrative of offence, disappointment, and anticipated distance. The behaviour is subtle: slower movements, quieter steps, a blankness around the eyes. There is no crisis. There is only repetition. The motif that threads through this subchapter—the trace line—helps clarify the process. A trace line is the faint but reliable path along which a reaction runs.

Show the sequence. Name its parts. Explain the mechanism. Follow the implication.

Every emotional loop begins with a cue, though the cue is often smaller than one expects: a delayed reply, a raised eyebrow, an unfinished sentence, a shift in someone's tone. The body responds before the mind interprets. Name the circuitry: the insula registers internal shifts; the amygdala scans for significance; the anterior cingulate monitors error. Explain the effect: these regions fire rapidly, sometimes within 200 milliseconds, shaping the meaning the mind will later attach. The implication is straightforward. If the first step is bodily, any meaningful attempt to understand a loop must begin by noticing the body.

This, however, is where many people falter. They try to analyse the story without observing the sensations that gave rise to it. They dissect the narrative—*Why do I think she's upset? Why does this matter so much?*—but ignore the tightening in their chest that set the tone. Honest mapping reverses the order: sensation first, story second.

Research supports this shift. A 2009 study at the University of California, Berkeley, led by Matthew Lieberman, found that participants who labelled their bodily sensations during an emotional stimulus showed reduced amygdala activation and increased activity in regions associated with conscious regulation. Behaviourally, they paused more often and responded with less urgency. The metric—reduction in physiological arousal—demonstrated that naming the body's response softened the loop's intensity. The implication is powerful: mapping sensations interrupts momentum.

A second, equally notable example comes from 2013 research at the University of Zurich, where researchers asked volunteers to describe not their emotions but the physical markers accompanying them. Participants who could specify sensations—"tightness behind ribs," "heat at the neck," "pressure on the forehead"—recovered more quickly from interpersonal stressors. Their visible behaviour: faster de-escalation in role-play conflicts. Their metric: reduced cortisol levels twenty minutes after the stressor. The explanation: embodied awareness breaks continuity between trigger and story. The implication: mapping is physiological as much as psychological.

Yet there is a credible limitation. Not everyone has equal access to interoceptive awareness. Individuals with certain trauma histories, as shown in studies led by Ruth Lanius at Western University (2010), often experience dampened signals from the body. Their behaviour may appear flat; their metrics show reduced insula activation. This does not undermine the role of mapping. It highlights that some must begin with noticing thoughts before sensations. Reconciliation lies in flexibility: the order matters less than the noticing itself.

Returning to Anna clarifies the mapping process. When she sits down later that evening with her journal, she does not analyse the friendship. Instead, she draws three short lines on the page titled: "Body," "Story," "Action." Under "Body", she writes: "Stomach dropped. Jaw tightened. Shoulders lifted." Under "Story": "She is disappointed. She is pulling away." Under "Action": "Cancelled my own plan for tomorrow. Went quiet." The journal entry is simple. The visible behaviour—writing concrete descriptions—anchors her attention. The trace line becomes clear. She sees the path her reaction travelled in real time.

This act of mapping aligns with older traditions. In the 13th century, the Sufi scholar Ibn Ata' Allah taught disciples to observe "the movements of the soul before the mind speaks." The instruction, though poetic, was behavioural: attend to micro-shifts before interpretation seizes control. Similarly, the *Examen* developed by Ignatius of Loyola in 1548 asked practitioners to review the day with special attention to bodily and emotional fluctuations. These traditions—despite differing metaphysics—recognised a shared truth: awareness precedes change.

Show why mapping matters. Name the outcome. Explain the transition. Follow the implication.

Mapping interrupts the loop by making the sequence explicit. Once the trace line is visible, a person can locate the point at which their reaction accelerates. For Anna, the acceleration occurs between sensation and story; the bodily drop is tolerable, but the instant leap to *I must have done something* shapes the rest. For others, acceleration may occur between story and action—moving too quickly to apology, withdrawal, or defensiveness.

The motif of the trace line appears again here. Without mapping, the line is blurred and feels inevitable. With mapping, the line becomes distinct—a route that could, with time, take a different direction.

Two more examples illustrate this. In 2017, a study at Stanford examined how people with habitual rumination responded to guided reflection. Participants who mapped their internal sequence, moment by moment, showed improved cognitive flexibility on follow-up tasks. Their behaviour: more willingness to revise initial interpretations. Their metric: increased performance on set-shifting tests. Implication: mapping loosens the grip of entrenched narratives.

In 2020, researchers at the University of Cambridge examined mapping practices among adolescents prone to emotional volatility. Those who articulated their triggers with specificity—rather than saying "I just lost it"—showed measurable reductions in reactive behaviour over six weeks. Behaviourally: fewer outbursts. Metric: reduced frequency by 23 per cent (Beckett et al., 2020). Explanation: self-awareness reconfigures prediction patterns in the brain. Implication: even young, rapidly shifting brains respond to mapping.

Yet one must address a limitation often raised by critics. Some fear that mapping becomes self-absorption—an inward spiral that distracts from action. There are cases where this happens, particularly when mapping is used to justify avoidance rather than transformation. But these are distortions. Proper mapping is descriptive, not indulgent. It does not ask *Why am I like this?* but *What happened inside me?* Reconciliation comes with discipline: mapping must remain factual, brief, and oriented toward clarity, not self-critique.

Returning one last time to Anna, the journal entry reveals something subtle: she notices that her story—*She is disappointed*—has appeared in dozens of interactions over the years. The behaviour is recognition: she underlines it twice. She then writes a question that marks the beginning of change: *Is this the only possible meaning?* That single question widens her mental field. The trace line bends slightly. And in that bending, the groove loosens.

We end, as this subchapter must, with a tension rather than resolution. Mapping reveals patterns. It shows where a reaction starts and how it travels. But once the map is drawn, the real question emerges: when the next trace line begins—when the stomach drops or the jaw tightens—will you follow the old route automatically, or pause long enough to ask what else the moment might hold?

Chapter 3
Meditation as Mental Weightlifting

On a cool morning in Kyoto in 1967, the Zen teacher Shunryu Suzuki watched a novice monk attempt his first seated meditation. The young man straightened his spine with almost military precision, fixed his gaze on the floor, and breathed as if performing for an examiner. Within minutes he began shifting, lowering one knee, then the other, as restlessness overtook determination. When the bell finally rang, he exhaled sharply, embarrassed by his own agitation. Suzuki simply smiled and said, "You have just met your mind." The remark did not chastise him; it named the universal experience of anyone who attempts to pay steady attention. Meditation was not meant to grant instant tranquillity. It was meant to reveal the raw material we are working with.

Most people imagine meditation as a serene refuge—soft light, poised posture, the mind resting in perfect stillness. The truth is closer to Suzuki's novice: distraction, adjustment, bodily whispers, sudden memories, spirals of planning, the itch on the shoulder that insists on being addressed. This is not failure. This is training. The mind wanders because that is what untrained attention does, especially in a world built to fracture it. The strength comes not from suppressing this wandering but from returning, again and again, with patient clarity. Each return is a repetition. Each repetition builds capacity. The motif that threads through this chapter—the repetition—captures it. Mental strength is not sculpted by dramatic breakthroughs but by the steady act of coming back.

If the previous chapter mapped how pain and habit carve grooves in the brain, this one examines how meditation begins to rewiring those grooves through deliberate practice. Attention becomes the weight we lift. Breath becomes the anchor we return to. Posture becomes the frame that steadies the nervous system. Every part of the practice, however ordinary it appears, has a corresponding shift in neural circuitry. And crucially, every moment of distraction is not merely an inconvenience but an opportunity: the exact spot where the neural fibres of regulation, perspective, and choice thicken.

The image of attention as a trainable muscle is not metaphor alone; it reflects measurable changes in the brain. Studies at Harvard in 2011 showed that eight weeks of focused attention practice increased cortical thickness in regions governing emotional regulation and working memory. Behaviourally, participants described quicker recovery from stress, clearer thinking, and a softer relationship with intrusive thoughts. These gains did not come from dramatic revelations during meditation sessions. They came from the mundane cycle experienced by every beginner: count three breaths, drift into a task list, remember the instructions, return. Count two breaths, slip into an argument replayed from last week, return. The repetition is the practice. The returning is the rewiring.

This chapter will explore that process in detail, but it begins by acknowledging a paradox: meditation promises peace yet introduces us, first, to discomfort. The discomfort is not punishment. It is data. It shows how scattered attention has become, how strongly habit pulls the mind into familiar ruts, and how resistant the brain can be to stillness. In a culture saturated with stimulation, silence can feel like deprivation. For someone accustomed to constant mental movement, sitting quietly can feel as unnatural as holding a plank position feels to someone unused to physical exertion. In both cases, strength emerges through repetition, not preference.

Consider a common scene: a parent, after settling children for the night, sits on the sofa to attempt ten minutes of breathing meditation. The house remains noisy—pipes clank, a neighbour closes a door, a phone vibrates somewhere under a cushion. Within seconds, the parent's mind leaps to next morning's commitments, then to an unresolved disagreement, then to a sudden fear that the laundry was left in the machine. Each distraction feels like a derailing. Yet each return to the breath—however brief—signals to the brain that attention can be reclaimed. What looks like a scattered session is, in fact, powerful conditioning. The mind wanders. The mind returns. The circuit strengthens.

Such ordinary scenes will shape the journey ahead in this chapter. Meditation does not occur in temples and monasteries alone. It occurs in bedrooms, office corridors, buses, parked cars, break rooms, and back gardens. It occurs in the ten minutes before a meeting or the five minutes after waking. It occurs amid noise, not despite it. And it is in these imperfect, ordinary conditions that the most meaningful neural changes begin. Meditation is less an escape from life than a rehearsal for meeting life with steadiness.

To understand why repetition matters so deeply, it helps to consider the mechanics of a simple practice. A ten-minute breathing meditation appears minimal in structure—sit upright, attend to breath, notice wandering, return. Yet each element recruits specific neural systems. Posture affects the vagus nerve, shifting the body toward parasympathetic regulation. Focusing on breath engages interoceptive circuits in the insula. Gently redirecting attention—without frustration—activates the prefrontal cortex, strengthening its regulatory influence over emotion-driven impulses. What feels "simple" is neurologically sophisticated. And precisely because it is simple, it can be repeated consistently, which is the key to rewiring.

But repetition only works if practitioners understand that wandering is not interruption. Wandering is the training stimulus. If attention were naturally steady, meditation would build nothing. The novice who counts "one, two, three, twelve, thirteen—wait—start again" is not doing the practice incorrectly. They are demonstrating its central principle: returning builds strength. Every rep counts, even messy ones. Especially messy ones.

This perspective reshapes how we interpret the common frustrations of meditation. The racing mind, the restless leg, the sudden flood of irritation—all are part of the weight being lifted. They reveal the habits that dominate mental life outside the practice. When someone wakes at 3 a.m. replaying a conversation, or spends an entire commute predicting the worst possible outcome, or feels overwhelmed after a single criticism, they are witnessing untrained attention pulled by old grooves. Meditation provides the laboratory where these grooves become visible, and through visibility, malleable.

Yet meditation is not merely a technique for relaxation, though relaxation may appear along the way. The deeper promise is clarity. Not mystical clarity, but perceptual clarity: the capacity to distinguish an emotion from the story attached to it, a thought from the reality it claims to describe, a worry from the event that triggered it. With practice, the practitioner begins to notice patterns hidden under daily momentum: the worry thought that always appears when silence lengthens, the irritation that masks anxiety, the sadness that surfaces after busyness drops away. These insights are not dramatic epiphanies. They are the quiet, cumulative recognitions that arise when the mind stops running long enough for its contents to settle into view.

Philosophical traditions across cultures understood this centuries before neuroscience began articulating it. In the Indian Buddhist text *Satipatthana Sutta* (1st century BCE), practitioners were instructed "to know the mind as the mind": a deceptively simple phrase that anticipates modern distinctions between awareness and thought content. In the writings of the Desert Fathers of the 4th century, monks described their practice as "watching the thoughts," noting the ones that returned repeatedly, especially during solitude. These ancient teachers recognised the same truth we now confirm through brain imaging: stillness allows the architecture of attention to become visible.

The relevance of meditation has only intensified in recent decades. With digital notifications multiplying, work and home boundaries blurring, and cognitive load increasing, focused attention has become a scarce resource. The modern nervous system, constantly tugged between tasks, rarely settles long enough to recover its baseline clarity. Meditation offers not nostalgic escape but necessary training: a deliberate counterweight to fragmentation.

Yet even as it becomes more popular, misunderstandings persist. Many assume meditation should quiet the mind instantly. Others assume it requires perfect conditions. Some believe they are "bad" at it because thoughts keep appearing. This chapter aims to dissolve such misconceptions by showing how meditation actually works: through repetition, through returning, through small acts of attentional strength that accumulate into significant change.

The scope ahead is clear. We will look at attention as a muscle—trainable, fatigable, strengthenable. We will break down the mechanics of a simple practice, illuminating why posture, breath, and redirection matter. We will examine the nature of wandering and reframe it as the heart of the discipline. And we will trace how sustained practice leads beyond momentary calm to structural clarity: the capacity to see one's patterns with greater precision and respond with greater freedom.

Yet beneath the technicalities lies a larger question: what kind of person emerges when attention becomes steady? What becomes possible when the mind no longer jerks toward fear, memory, or prediction the moment silence appears? When returning becomes instinct rather than effort?

That is the horizon this chapter points toward. The path begins not with mastery, but with the humble, repeated act Suzuki recognised in his novice: noticing the mind, meeting it as it is, and returning—patiently, gently, again.

Attention as a Trainable Muscle

In November 1894, at the University of Leipzig, Wilhelm Wundt asked a group of students to perform what seemed an absurdly simple task. They were to watch a small black dot on a rotating drum and press a key whenever their attention drifted. Wundt expected occasional lapses. Instead, he recorded more than forty in the first three minutes. One participant, Ernst Meumann, confessed afterwards that he was shocked by the weakness of his own concentration: "I could not hold one dot still in my mind." Wundt's notes captured a truth that remains intact across a century of research: attention, left untrained, behaves like an unconditioned muscle. It flickers. It fatigues. It wanders. And yet—crucially—it can be strengthened.

A scene far from Leipzig illustrates the same principle. Picture Maya, a solicitor in Bristol, sitting on her sofa before work, attempting her first session of breath-counting meditation. She inhales gently—one. Exhales—two. On the fourth breath she remembers an email she forgot to send. She resets—one. She reaches three, then drifts into planning dinner. She resets again. Within five minutes she has restarted more times than she cares to admit. Her visible behaviour—shuffling her posture, glancing at the clock, sighing quietly—reveals a familiar struggle. Yet beneath the discomfort lies something important. Each return, however clumsy, is a repetition. Each repetition strengthens a circuit. Just as a novice's limbs tremble during early weightlifting sessions, a novice meditator's attention trembles under the weight of stillness. The trembling is not failure. It is training.

The motif that threads through this subchapter—the rep—captures the heart of the matter. Attention grows through reps, not through ideal conditions or innate talent. The rep is the cycle of wandering and returning, the movement from distraction back to anchor, repeated enough times to carve new pathways in the brain.

Show the process. Name the networks. Explain the mechanism. Follow the implications.

Attention is not a singular faculty but a system. Neuroscientists describe at least two major networks: the *default mode network* (DMN), which generates spontaneous thoughts, and the *frontal-parietal control network* (FPCN), which directs focus deliberately. When Maya attempts to count her breaths, the DMN offers memories, plans, worries, and half-formed ideas; the FPCN attempts to steer her back. The visible behaviour—her resetting the count after drifting—marks the moment the FPCN re-engages. The more often this happens, the stronger the regulatory circuits become.

Evidence for this training effect is both historical and contemporary. In 1972, at the University of Wisconsin–Madison, Lawrence Shapiro documented that participants who practised daily concentration exercises for six weeks could maintain focus on a simple target for triple their baseline duration. Their behaviour changed measurably: fewer fidgeting movements, slower eye blinks, steadier breathing. Decades later, in 2011, a team at Harvard led by Sara Lazar used MRI scans to show increased cortical thickness in the left hippocampus and posterior cingulate cortex after eight weeks of mindfulness training. These regions govern learning, memory, and attention regulation. The implication is clear. Attention practice reshapes structure.

A second, equally instructive example comes from 2018 research at the University of Cambridge. Children who practised brief attentional games for just ten minutes a day over four weeks showed improved performance on sustained attention tasks. Their behaviour—fewer errors of omission—indicated sharper focus. The metric—reaction-time variability—reduced significantly. The explanation: repetition strengthened top-down control. The implication: the attention-muscle metaphor holds across ages and environments.

Yet limitations matter. Not everyone responds to training at the same pace. Individuals with chronic stress, ADHD, or sleep deprivation may find their minds wander more frequently and return more slowly. This does not contradict the training principle; it highlights the need for realistic expectations. A fatigued nervous system lifts lighter weights. A rested one lifts more.

Returning to Maya, her ellipsis of lapses is not a sign of inadequacy but the raw data of her brain learning to regulate itself. When she reaches "five" without drifting, even once, that rep has strengthened a neural fibre. When she notices she has wandered after a full minute—rather than falling into a ten-minute daydream—that noticing is itself progress. Growth reveals itself in brevity: shorter drift, faster return.

Show why wandering happens. Name the driver. Explain its function. Follow the implication.

The mind wanders because it evolved to monitor multiple streams of information. Early humans needed to look for predators, remember routes, anticipate weather shifts, and track social dynamics. Wandering was adaptive. Modern life, however, floods the mind with more stimuli than it can track meaningfully. When Maya sits quietly, the DMN continues generating content as though continuing its scanning role, but without an external target. A worry about tomorrow's meeting has the same neural signature as the rustle in the bushes once did: a potential threat to be explored. The implication is counterintuitive: wandering is normal, but untrained wandering becomes intrusive.

Training attention does not eradicate wandering; it shifts the balance between networks. MRI studies from 2016 at Stanford show that experienced meditators do not eliminate DMN activity; they strengthen connectivity between the FPCN and DMN, allowing quicker recognition of drifting and smoother redirection. Their behaviour during tasks—calmer posture, slower speech, reduced startle reflex—reflects this internal coordination.

The motif of the rep returns. Every redirection is a rep. Without redirection, no growth occurs.

One might ask: if attention can be trained like muscle, what exactly is strengthened? The answer lies in two intertwined competencies: *stability* and *meta-awareness*. Stability is the capacity to hold attention on a chosen object—breath, sound, posture—for increasing durations. Meta-awareness is the ability to notice distraction without fusing with it. These qualities combine to create attentional strength.

Show stability in practice. Name the anchor. Explain its effect. Follow the implication.

When Maya counts her breaths, she uses the breath as an anchor—a simple, rhythmic object that stabilises attention. Anchors work because they are continuous, neutral, and always present. Behaviourally, they produce small changes: slower respiration, relaxed facial muscles, steadier gaze. Neurologically, they activate interoceptive pathways through the insula, grounding the mind in bodily sensation rather than conceptual drift. The implication: with enough reps, the mind learns to rest on the anchor with less effort.

Show meta-awareness. Name its trigger. Explain its effect. Follow the implication.

Meta-awareness arises the moment Maya realises she has been distracted. The behaviour is microscopic: a softening of expression, a quiet mental note—*thinking*. That note activates the dorsolateral prefrontal cortex and dampens amygdala-driven impulses. The implication: noticing a thought creates distance from it. That distance is the foundation of choice.

Historical sources reinforce these insights. In the *Visuddhimagga*, a 5th-century Buddhist meditation manual, practitioners are instructed to "know the mind wandering as wandering, and the mind returning as returning." The behaviour—naming the movement—mirrors modern cognitive strategies. Similarly, in 14th-century Christian hesychast texts, monks were taught to "bring back the mind as it flees." The repetition—returning twenty, fifty, a hundred times—was their rep. Across cultures, the principle stands: attention strengthens through recall, not rigidity.

A key question arises: what counts as progress? The beginner often seeks long stretches of perfect stillness. But the real metric is frequency of return, not duration of unbroken focus. If Maya wanders thirty times in ten minutes but notices twenty of them, she has performed twenty reps of attentional lifting. If she wanders only five times but notices none until the bell rings, she has performed zero reps. The implication challenges common assumptions: a "messy" meditation may be more neurologically fruitful than a "calm" one.

A credible counter-example illustrates this nuance. Some long-term practitioners in monastic environments report entering states of deep absorption where wandering nearly disappears. Their behaviour during these states—slowed pulse, serene posture—suggests heightened parasympathetic activity. Does this contradict the rep-based model? No. It represents advanced conditioning. The rep phase built the muscle; the absorption phase reflects its strength. Without thousands of early reps, such depth would not arise.

Returning again to Maya: after two weeks of daily practice, she notices subtle changes. She catches her mind drifting during a meeting and returns to the speaker within seconds rather than minutes. She interrupts fewer conversations. She walks to the train with more presence. These are the behavioural markers of strengthened attention. They are small, yet they matter. Attention trained in one domain transfers to others.

Two further examples deepen the point. In 2009, researchers at Oxford found that individuals practising focused attention meditation made fewer errors in the Sustained Attention to

Response Task (SART). Their behaviour—more consistent keypress intervals—showed improved vigilance. The metric: reduction in attentional lapses by 30 per cent (Jha et al., 2009). Implication: reps translate into measurable performance.

In 2021, a study at the University of Toronto observed that even short bursts of attentional practice (five minutes, three times per day) improved selective attention in adults under high workload. Behaviourally: fewer task-switching costs. Metric: improved Stroop test performance. Implication: small, frequent reps accumulate meaningfully.

Limitations persist, of course. Fatigue, trauma, chronic anxiety, and severe stress zones create conditions where attention wavers more and returns more slowly. These conditions do not make practice futile; they make it more necessary. A weakened muscle does not require abandonment; it requires smaller reps and longer rest.

The motif of the rep appears one last time. Meditation is not a pursuit of stillness but a willingness to train with wandering. Every return is a rep. Every rep is a thread. Threads weave into pathways. Pathways, strengthened, become choices.

Which leads to the unresolved question at the heart of this subchapter: if attention can be trained one rep at a time, what might your mind become capable of when returning—not drifting—becomes the more familiar path?

The Mechanics of a Simple Practice

In January 1965, at the Massachusetts General Hospital in Boston, a young cardiologist named Herbert Benson noticed an anomaly. Patients practising a basic breathing technique—learned not from medical textbooks but from two visiting practitioners of Transcendental Meditation—showed measurable drops in oxygen consumption within minutes. Benson repeated the experiment with laboratory controls. The data held. Blood pressure lowered. Heart rate steadied. A small, almost austere practice produced physiological outcomes that standard interventions had failed to shift. The scene became a quiet landmark in the scientific study of contemplative training: a reminder that simple, repeatable actions—posture, breath, attention—can alter the body's deepest rhythms.

Half a century later, on an ordinary morning in Manchester, a postgraduate student named Aaron attempts his first structured breathing meditation. He sits on the edge of his bed, straightens his back reflexively, and realises within seconds that he has no idea where to place his hands. He experiments—on knees? in lap? one over the other?—and chooses the least awkward. He closes his eyes. Breath enters through his nose, cool and thin. He counts one. Breath leaves, warm, slower. He counts two. By six, he is wondering whether he should be feeling "calm" by now. By ten, he remembers a message he forgot to answer. His posture wilts. His attention scatters. And yet, if he could see inside his brain, he would witness something quietly remarkable: circuits recruiting, networks shifting, a fragile but genuine act of training taking place.

Every simple practice begins like this—with uncertainty, awkward posture, wandering thoughts. Yet it is precisely in these unremarkable moments that the mechanics of meditation reveal their depth. The motif that threads through this subchapter—the frame—captures it. Posture frames attention. Breath frames sensation. Redirection frames choice. These frames, repeated, become structure.

Show the posture. Name the system it influences. Explain the mechanism. Follow the implication.

A stable posture does not exist for aesthetic reasons. It shapes the body's regulatory systems. When Aaron lifts his spine gently, he elongates the vagus nerve pathway running from the brainstem through the torso. This subtle action—barely perceptible in behaviour—enhances parasympathetic tone. The parasympathetic system, responsible for "rest-and-digest" responses, lowers heart rate and softens muscular tension. Studies from 2007 at the University of North Carolina found that upright but relaxed sitting increased vagal tone even before meditation began. The implication is straightforward: posture is physiology. A slumped frame reinforces lethargy and rumination; an upright frame signals readiness and stability.

Benson's early images demonstrated a related phenomenon: consistent posture stabilises breathing patterns, which in turn stabilise neural firing in regions tied to emotional processing. To put it plainly: how you sit shapes how you feel. Sitting becomes the first frame.

Show the anchor. Name the circuit. Explain its role. Follow the implication.

The breath serves as the most universal anchor not for symbolic reasons, but for neurological ones. Breathing rhythm activates interoceptive pathways in the insular cortex—the region responsible for sensing internal states. When Aaron pays attention to the sensation of breath entering the nostrils or lifting the diaphragm, he is engaging those pathways. The behaviour is trivial: noticing air. Yet the effect is concrete. Interoceptive attention dampens activity in the default mode network (DMN), the cluster of regions associated with self-referential thinking, mind-wandering, and worry. Evidence from Richard Davidson's lab in 2012 showed that focusing on breath reduces DMN activation even in novices.

The implication is significant. An anchor is not chosen for poetic value; it is chosen because it consistently recruits circuits that calm narrative rumination. The anchor becomes the second frame.

Show the redirection. Name the network. Explain the change. Follow the implication.

The gentle act of returning attention to the breath after drifting engages executive control circuits—most notably the dorsolateral prefrontal cortex (DLPFC). When Aaron realises his mind has wandered to his unanswered message and brings it back to counting, he is recruiting top-down regulation. That tiny behaviour—the inward pivot—strengthens synaptic connections between the DLPFC and subcortical regions tied to emotional arousal. Repeated often enough, this "return" becomes a conditioned response. The implication is quietly transformative: the more one practises returning in meditation, the easier it becomes to return to composure during stress.

A limitation deserves acknowledgement. Those experiencing trauma, acute anxiety, or chronic exhaustion may find breath-based concentration overwhelming. In such cases, focusing stabilises more slowly. Yet this does not negate the mechanics; it reveals the nervous system's sensitivity. The frame must be lighter, the anchor gentler, the redirection softer.

Before expanding the deeper dynamics, it is helpful to walk through a ten-minute script—not as instruction, but as a window into what a simple practice actually feels like from the inside. Imagine Aaron attempting it.

Sit comfortably, with your back upright but not rigid. Let your hands rest wherever they fall naturally. Notice the points of contact—feet on floor, legs on chair, hands touching legs. Allow the face to soften. Feel the gentle pull of gravity on the shoulders.

Bring attention to your breath. Do not change its rhythm. Notice where it is easiest to feel—in the nostrils, the chest, or the abdomen. Choose that spot lightly. Breathe in, aware of the in-breath. Breathe out, aware of the out-breath.

Begin to count each exhalation. One. Two. Three. When the mind wanders—as it will—note that it has wandered and return to 'one'. If frustration appears, notice it as another moment of wandering. Return again.

After several minutes, release the counting. Remain with the raw sensation of breath. Let experience unfold without interference. If sound arises, note sound. If thought arises, note thought. Return gently whenever pulled.

In the final minute, widen awareness to the body as a whole. Notice warmth, pressure, stillness. End the session by inhaling once deeply, exhaling slowly, and opening the eyes.

What appears unremarkable on the surface is, beneath it, a series of neurobiological shifts. Sitting upright modulates vagal tone. Breath attention activates interoception. Counting imposes a cognitive frame that interrupts rumination. Returning strengthens top-down regulation. Each of these steps is simple enough to seem inconsequential, yet layered enough to produce structural change.

Historical sources reinforce the importance of such simplicity. In the *Anapanasati Sutta* (1st century BCE), practitioners were instructed to "know the breath long as long, short as short," reflecting an early understanding that sensing breath directly sharpens interoceptive precision. In 13th-century Japanese Zen texts, Dōgen wrote that meditation required "just sitting"—shikantaza—yet the discipline of "just" sitting demanded exquisite care in posture and breath. These traditions recognised what neuroscience now confirms: simplicity enables precision. Precision enables consistency. Consistency enables change.

To show the significance of this consistency, consider two case studies. In 2014, researchers at the University of Wisconsin conducted an eight-week study on employees at a biotechnology company, Promega Corporation, in Madison. Participants practised ten minutes of breath-focused meditation daily. Behaviourally, they showed lower startle responses and improved concentration at work. Physiologically, they demonstrated reduced inflammatory markers. The implication: even minimal daily practice alters both mind and body.

A second example comes from 2019 work at the University of Queensland. Students practising breath counting for ten minutes a day over six weeks showed improved performance on attention-switching tasks. Their reaction-time variability decreased. The implication: a simple anchor—breath—can translate into broader cognitive flexibility.

Yet meditation's apparent simplicity often misleads beginners. They imagine that counting should immediately quieten thought. When distraction persists, they assume failure. But distraction is not an obstacle; it is the training stimulus. The motif of the frame returns here: the frame does not remove the content inside it; it holds it. Breath holds wandering. Posture holds agitation. Redirection holds doubt. Meditation is not content-free; it is framed content.

Show the wandering. Name the driver. Explain its role. Follow the implication.

Wandering arises from the default mode network—an engine that produces memories, predictions, wishes, regrets. When Aaron drifts into imagining his next presentation, he is experiencing this system at full strength. The DMN is not a flaw; it is part of the brain's meaning-making apparatus. But when it dominates unchallenged, attention becomes hostage to habit. The implication: meditation is not the suppression of wandering but the rebalancing of networks.

This rebalancing yields perceptual clarity. When Aaron notices a thought—not as truth but as thought—he creates distance between stimulus and reaction. That distance is the raw material of choice. Choice, repeated, becomes agency.

A credible counter-example shows the subtlety of this process. Some people report that focusing on breath intensifies anxiety or triggers panic. Behaviourally, their breathing becomes shallow; their posture tightens. Neurologically, the amygdala surges. Does this invalidate the mechanics? No. It indicates that breath, as an anchor, is too direct for a destabilised nervous system. Anchors must meet the practitioner where they are. For such individuals, sound or touch may be gentler. The mechanics remain the same; the tool adjusts.

Returning to the motif: the frame. Posture frames intention. Breath frames presence. Redirection frames resilience. These frames become internal architecture.

The subchapter closes by turning toward a practical tension. If a simple practice can alter neural pathways so effectively, why do so many people struggle to maintain consistency? What prevents the frame from becoming a habit rather than an aspiration?

The answer points forward. Will you treat the mechanics—posture, breath, return—as a one-time experiment, or will you commit to them as a daily frame? The quality of your attention depends on that choice.

What Happens When the Mind Wanders

In November 2010, at Harvard University in Cambridge, psychologist Matthew Killingsworth published a result that surprised even seasoned researchers. Using real-time reports from thousands of people via smartphone prompts, he found that human minds were not focused on what they were doing for almost 47 per cent of their waking lives (Killingsworth & Gilbert, *Science*, 2010). People reported attention drifting during work, conversation, eating, commuting, even during activities they enjoyed. A paradox emerged: the more the mind wandered, the less content people tended to feel. Yet mind-wandering was not an occasional glitch. It was the default. One short sentence captures the tension. *The mind leaves before we notice.*

This tension becomes particularly vivid when someone attempts meditation in ordinary conditions. Imagine Leila, a secondary school teacher in Birmingham, sitting on a cushion in her living room at 6.30 a.m. The radiator clicks. A lorry reverses outside with a long mechanical beep. Her neighbour's door slams. Upstairs, her younger child turns over in bed and thumps the wall. Leila places her hands on her knees, closes her eyes, and begins to follow her breath. Within seconds she is thinking about lesson plans, then yesterday's argument, then the packed lunches she may have forgotten to finish. She catches herself, returns to the breath, and a moment later is pulled by the sound of a bin truck on the street. Part of her concludes, "I can't meditate in this house." Yet, viewed more closely, something else is happening: each time she notices the drift and returns, she is performing the core movement that strengthens attention. The noise is not ruining the practice. It *is* the practice.

The motif that threads through this subchapter is simple: *the return.* Wandering is the movement away. The return is the hinge between impulse and training. Without wandering, there would be nothing to return *from.* Without return, wandering would simply continue as before. Meditation lives in that hinge.

Show the wandering. Name the system. Explain its function. Follow the implication.

When Leila sits, the default mode network—the brain's narrative generator—continues its work unabated. The DMN stitches together memories, plans, self-evaluations, imagined conversations. It is the same system that Killingsworth's study indirectly illuminated: the wandering mind as constant storyteller. Behaviourally, its activity shows up as thought streams: replaying yesterday's comment, predicting the headteacher's response, rehearsing an email. The DMN is not pathological; it supports imagination and planning. But when unregulated, it hijacks attention even in moments explicitly dedicated to quiet. The implication is crucial. Wandering during meditation does not signal that something has gone uniquely wrong. It reveals that the same network that dominates ordinary life has followed the practitioner onto the cushion.

Show the moment of noticing. Name the regulatory network. Explain the shift. Follow the implication.

The first time Leila realises she has stopped feeling her breath and started planning lessons, another network engages: the frontoparietal control network, including the dorsolateral prefrontal cortex. Behaviourally, this is almost invisible—a flicker of awareness, a silent mental note: *Thinking*. That tiny moment is the return. It represents top-down regulation asserting itself over automatic narrative flow. In 2011, Judson Brewer and colleagues at Yale used fMRI scans to show that experienced meditators exhibit increased coupling between attention-regulating regions and the DMN when instructed to notice mind-wandering (Brewer et al., *PNAS*, 2011). The brain of a trained practitioner does not stop producing thoughts; it becomes more efficient at recognising and releasing them. The implication: the quality of meditation is not measured by absence of wandering but by frequency and gentleness of return.

This re-framing matters because many beginners interpret wandering as evidence of defect. They imagine that "real" meditators sit in pristine stillness, free of distraction. Historical sources disagree. In the 4th century, the Desert Father Evagrius Ponticus catalogued *logismoi*—recurring thought patterns that besieged monks at prayer. Rather than treating them as proof of failure, he described them as material for discernment. In effect, he was saying: *Expect wandering; work with the return.*

To see how this plays out in a noisy house, follow Leila through ten minutes. She sits. Breath. Door slam. Mind leaps: *He's going to wake the baby.* She notices the thought, feels tension in her shoulders, returns to the breath. Two breaths later, the lorry beeps again. Her mind replies: *I hate this street.* She notices the resentment, feels heat in her throat, returns. Three breaths later, she remembers a marking deadline. She spins through a silent list, feels her chest constrict, returns. The behaviour is repetitive: leaving and coming back. If she were wired to a scanner, we would likely see DMN activity spike, then prefrontal regions engage, then interoceptive regions (insula) light as breath re-enters awareness. The implication is that each circuit of this loop is a *rep* in mental training. Noise provides resistance, like weight on a barbell.

At this point a limitation arises. Some situations overload the system. For individuals with severe trauma histories or very high arousal, certain kinds of wandering—particularly into intrusive memories—may exceed what self-guided meditation can safely hold. Their behaviour during such episodes—rapid breathing, dissociation, sudden panic—indicates a nervous system in flood. Acknowledging this does not invalidate the central principle; it contextualises it. The return is still the training hinge, but the anchor and environment may need to be adapted in consultation with appropriate support. The mind cannot train under weights that break rather than strengthen.

Within a workable range of difficulty, however, wandering is precisely where resilience is built. Resilience here is not a vague trait; it is the capacity of attention to reorient under stress. Two empirical examples illustrate this.

In 2012, a University of Wisconsin–Madison study followed participants on an eight-week mindfulness course. In the final session they completed a Sustained Attention to Response Task under deliberately distracting conditions: random sounds, flashing images, intermittent prompts. Those who had practised recognising and returning from mind-wandering showed fewer commission errors and quicker recovery after distractions. Their behaviour under pressure—shorter reaction-time spikes—demonstrated trained reorientation. The implication: noticing and returning in meditation translates into performance when life becomes noisy.

In 2016, researchers at the University of Exeter studied adults with recurrent depression engaging in mindfulness-based cognitive therapy. Participants learned to notice rumination and bring attention back to bodily sensation. Over months, many reported that while ruminative chains still began automatically, they could interrupt them earlier. Behaviourally: fewer "lost hours" of looping thought. Metric: reduced relapse rates over the following year. The wandering mind did not vanish, but the response to wandering changed.

The motif of *the return* appears in both cases. Training does not consist of preventing mind-wandering. It consists of shortening its unattended duration.

This has an immediate spiritual implication. Many traditions speak of "remembering" the sacred, the ethical, or the meaningful after forgetting. The Islamic word *dhikr* literally means remembrance; Christian contemplatives speak of recollection. The assumption is not perpetual awareness but repeated returning. Meditation makes that structure explicit at the neural level. Each breath noticed after distraction is a tiny act of remembrance: of presence, of choice, of values.

The noisy house vignette demonstrates another vital function of wandering: it reveals our most rehearsed concerns. When external sound pulls Leila's attention, it rarely pulls it into neutral territory. It latches onto pre-existing grooves: worrying about her child's sleep, resenting the lorry, fearing professional failure. The content of wandering is diagnostic. It answers a simple question: *When the mind has nothing assigned to it, where does it go?* Over weeks of practice, practitioners begin to recognise the greatest hits of their personal soundtrack—particular worries that recur, particular stories that resurface amid silence. This recognition is not yet liberation, but it is accurate mapping.

A counter-example clarifies the distinction between helpful observation and unhelpful indulgence. Someone might argue: "If I keep noticing my worries, am I not reinforcing them?" It depends on how the noticing occurs. When wandering slides into rumination, the person fuses with the thought—"This will go badly"—and elaborates it. Behaviourally: frowning, shallow breathing, time passing unnoticed. In contrast, when wandering is noticed as *wandering*, the practitioner labels the event ("worrying"), feels the associated sensation, and returns to the anchor. Behaviourally: brief pause, perhaps a deeper breath, then reorientation. The thought receives less fuel. Over time, its intensity often diminishes. The same neural content appears, but its reinforcement pattern changes.

Here again, Brewer's 2011 study is instructive. Experienced meditators shown emotionally charged images displayed reduced activation in the posterior cingulate cortex—associated with getting "caught up" in self-referential processing—when they applied awareness to their reactions. They still perceived the images. They simply related to them differently. The return altered the loop.

The motif of *the return* reappears if we watch Leila months later. The house is no quieter. Radiator, lorry, door, footsteps: all still there. Her mind still wanders. But now the arc of wandering is shorter. She might notice, "Annoyance," and feel it as heat before it grows into a full internal complaint. She might catch "Planning" before the list becomes a spiral. She still leaves the breath. She simply comes back sooner, and with slightly more kindness. The resilience is not in never being pulled; it is in the reliability of her return.

There is a further implication, more subtle and more spiritual. Each return is an implicit statement about what one takes to be central. When a person returns to the breath after being absorbed in resentment, they enact a micro-choice: present-moment sensation over habitual grievance. When they return from anxious rehearsal to the feeling of sitting, they choose actuality over prediction. Over time, these micro-choices accumulate into a different sense of who is in charge. The "I" that returns begins to feel more trustworthy than the "I" swept along by every passing thought.

Yet the practice also poses a difficult question, one that sits at the edge of this subchapter. If wandering is inevitable, and returning is the core of training, what does it mean to orient a whole life around the return rather than around the content of distraction? Put more plainly: when the mind wanders for half of each day, which half will you commit to training—the half that drifts, or the half that comes back?

Beyond Calm: Clarity and Insight

In April 1979, at the University of Massachusetts Medical School in Worcester, Jon Kabat-Zinn observed something unexpected. Participants in his fledgling Stress Reduction Clinic—many referred by physicians after months of chronic pain—reported not only moments of calm but sudden flashes of understanding about their own behaviour. One patient described it as "seeing the machinery of my reactions," another as "catching myself before I go off." These remarks were not about serenity. They were about clarity. Kabat-Zinn later wrote that meditation revealed "the landscape of the mind itself," a phrase that signalled a wider shift: contemplative practice was beginning to show that its deepest effects were cognitive, not merely soothing.

Nearly half a century later, clarity still arrives in modest, almost domestic moments. Imagine Daniel, an accountant in Leeds, sitting at his kitchen table at 7.00 p.m. attempting his evening practice. His phone buzzes on the counter. He has promised not to look. He focuses on his breath. Within seconds, a familiar worry thought appears with its usual force: *I'm falling behind at work*. It lands with such immediacy that he feels his stomach tighten. Five minutes later it appears again, almost identically. Ten minutes later, again. By the end of the session Daniel notices something not exactly profound, yet quietly disruptive: the worry feels formulaic, like a script performed by an actor trying too hard. The thought has not disappeared. But its authority has shifted. It looks less like truth and more like habit. A small shift, yes, but a clear one. And clarity, once tasted, rarely stays passive.

The motif that threads through this subchapter is *the glimpse*: the brief, precise moment when the mind sees its own pattern. A glimpse is not dramatic. It is not enlightenment. It is a clean view—uncovered, unforced—of what usually operates unseen.

Show the difference. Name the networks involved. Explain the shift. Follow the implication.

Relaxation and clarity share a surface, but they rest on different foundations. Relaxation arises when the parasympathetic nervous system engages: heart rate slows, muscle tension decreases, cortisol levels fall. This explains why many novices feel lighter after even five minutes of breath awareness. Behaviourally: shoulders drop, breath lengthens, eyes soften.

Clarity emerges elsewhere. It depends on strengthened interaction between the prefrontal cortex—responsible for executive regulation—and the insula, which tracks internal states. MRI research from 2016 at Stanford University revealed that sustained mindfulness training led to increased connectivity between these regions when participants observed thoughts without judgement. The behaviour associated with clarity is not softer muscles but quicker recognition: a thought seen as thought, an emotion identified before it becomes behaviour. The implication is profound. Calm alters state. Clarity alters perspective.

Consider a historical analogue. In 12th-century Japan, the Zen master Dōgen wrote that meditation "turns the light inward," a phrase often misread as mystical. In context, it meant something far more practical: *the mind becomes able to observe itself without distortion.* That description anticipates what modern neuroscience now measures—decreased activation in circuits tied to self-referential grip (posterior cingulate cortex) when practitioners apply awareness to thought flow. The frame may be ancient, but the mechanics are present.

Show the hidden pattern. Name the assumption. Explain its hold. Follow the implication.

Returning to Daniel: his recurring thought—*I'm falling behind*—is not random. It embodies an assumption: productivity equals security. That assumption, rehearsed for years, has carved a groove in his neural circuitry. Behaviourally, it appears as compulsive checking of emails, difficulty resting even when exhausted, and a tightening of the jaw when imagining deadlines. When Daniel sees the thought's repetitiveness during meditation, he glimpses its constructed nature. The thought has been masquerading as fact. Meditation reveals it as habit.

Two real-world examples deepen this point.

In 2010, researchers at UCLA studied long-term meditators and noted increased thickness in the temporoparietal junction—an area implicated in perspective-taking. Participants reported noticing "implicit beliefs" during meditation more readily than before. Behaviourally: reduced reactivity in social conflict, improved decision-making under pressure. The implication: clarity begins with seeing assumptions rather than acting from them.

In 2018, at the University of Zurich, researchers studying mindfulness-based interventions for anxiety found participants frequently reported recognising "the first link in the chain"—the earliest moment of worry forming. This early detection correlated with reduced physiological arousal on skin conductance measures. Again, the implication holds: clarity interrupts escalation.

A limitation is worth acknowledging. Not all insights that appear in meditation are reliable. The mind can produce distorted interpretations, especially under fatigue or emotional strain. Someone might misread a bodily sensation as a revelation or interpret a passing image as a call to action. Behaviourally, such misreadings show as impulsive decisions during or immediately after practice. This does not invalidate the pursuit of clarity. It highlights the necessity of grounding each glimpse in consistent observation over time rather than in momentary intensity.

Show the emotional pattern. Name the trigger. Explain the cycle. Follow the implication.

Meditation often reveals not individual thoughts but whole emotional arcs. For example, someone may notice that irritation always appears seconds before sadness, or that anxiety reliably precedes over-planning. These micro-sequences—usually invisible in daily life—come into view in the stillness of practice. They reveal that emotions do not arrive fully formed; they unfold. Behaviourally: a slight tension in the throat before anger, a micro-frown before worry, a collapse of posture before resignation. The implication is liberating. Once an emotional pattern is seen in its early stages, it becomes easier to interrupt.

A case study illustrates this clearly. In 2014, at the University of Toronto, participants in a mindfulness and affect-labelling study were asked to identify emotions in real time during meditation. Over weeks, many reported recognising emotional patterns earlier than before. Physiologically, their heart-rate variability improved—a marker of enhanced emotional regulation. The glimpse of pattern preceded the shift in behaviour.

Returning to Daniel's practice, clarity arrives not when he stops worrying but when he sees the worry *as a loop*. During meditation he notices: the worry appears, tightens his stomach, triggers a mental image of his overflowing inbox, and then dissolves as attention returns to breath. Ten minutes later, the same cycle replays almost identically. This repetition is the glimpse. The mind is reenacting a script. And seeing the script is the beginning of loosening it.

The motif of *the glimpse* appears again when Daniel sits a week later. This time, the worry thought arises with slightly less intensity. He recognises it quicker. It still tightens his stomach, but the sensation softens sooner. His behavioural markers shift: less fidgeting, fewer deep sighs, more fluidity between breath and awareness. The worry has not vanished. Its hold has weakened.

Show the deeper movement. Name the cognitive shift. Explain the difference. Follow the implication.

Clarity involves a move from identification to observation. Identification sounds like: "I am behind." Observation sounds like: "The thought about being behind has appeared." This linguistic shift mirrors a neural one: increased activation in regions associated with meta-awareness and decreased activation in regions tied to emotional fusion. The behaviour shows up subtly: a pause before reacting, a softening of tone during stress, a willingness to examine rather than obey a thought.

Two additional examples show the practical consequences of this shift.

At the University of Sussex in 2013, researchers observed that participants trained in open monitoring meditation were more likely to catch cognitive biases during decision-making tasks. They paused longer before confirming an initial instinct and corrected errors more often. Behaviourally: fewer snap judgements. Implication: clarity alters thought evaluation.

In 2017, a study at Oxford found that individuals practising daily mindfulness noticed catastrophic thoughts ("Everything will go wrong") more quickly and labelled them as mental events rather than truths. Over three months, participants showed reduced behavioural avoidance and improved problem-solving. The implication: clarity empowers more nuanced action.

The motif of the glimpse returns once more. The glimpse is not a peak experience but a tiny interval of recognition. Its power lies in repetition. With each glimpse, the practitioner sees more clearly the architecture of their reactions. Over time, the mind becomes less compelled by its own content.

But clarity also introduces a tension, one that invites genuine reflection. If calm offers temporary relief while clarity offers structural transformation, which is the real purpose of meditation? The pleasant state or the penetrating insight? The ease of relaxation or the discomfort of seeing oneself accurately?

Meditation answers the tension by asking another question: when a recurring thought appears tomorrow—perhaps Daniel's *I'm falling behind*, perhaps yours—will you relate to it as truth, or will you recognise its shape? Only one of those responses leads to freedom.

Chapter 4
Training the Heart: Compassion and the Social Brain

On a damp Wednesday evening in Glasgow, the McLeod household reached boiling point over something as trivial as a missing set of keys. Voices rose, doors thudded, and a tension—thick, metallic, unmistakable—settled over the kitchen. Ten minutes later, no one could recall what the original spark had been. But each person could feel, in their own body, the aftershocks: a tight jaw, a quickened pulse, eyes slightly harder than usual. When their teenage son entered the room, cheerful from football practice, the mood hit him like a weather front. His shoulders lifted; his smile dimmed; the brightness drained from his voice. No one had spoken to him harshly. Yet something in the air had already done the work. This is what it means to live with a social brain. Moods—like heat or cold—radiate.

We pretend otherwise, of course. We talk about "my emotions," as if feelings were private possessions sealed behind the ribs. But the nervous system is porous. It mirrors what it encounters. It absorbs. It attunes. In a household under strain, the nervous systems of its members begin to tune to the same frequency, often without any conscious intention. Neuroscientists have known this for years: mirror neurons fire when we watch another person act; limbic resonance transmits anxiety or calm across the thin space between bodies; facial micro-expressions subtly steer emotional states in those who witness them. A single argument, even about keys, can ripple through a family's physiology long after the heat of the moment has passed.

The paradox is stark. We are wired to connect, yet the very wiring that makes connection possible also makes us exquisitely vulnerable to one another. A sharp sigh from a colleague, a raised eyebrow from a partner, the clipped tone of a stranger on public transport—each can shift our internal state before our conscious mind has registered the event. And when we endure isolation, chronic conflict, or relationships haunted by unspoken fear, those same social circuits begin to misfire. The nervous system braces, scanning for danger even in safe places. The body becomes an instrument tuned too tightly.

This chapter steps into that fragile, ordinary terrain—the realm of relationships, not as sentimental ideal but as neurological reality. Compassion, here, is not the soft virtue of greeting-card philosophy. It is a radical recalibration of the social brain. It is skill, signal, and rewiring all at once: a deliberate shift from self-protection to softening, from reactivity to receptivity, from habitual suspicion to grounded openness.

Consider a scene in an office in Sheffield. Two colleagues, Martina and Rowan, disagree sharply in a morning meeting. Rowan's tone is firm to the point of curt. Martina feels her chest tighten, her breath rise, her shoulders angle defensively. She recognises the familiar pattern: retreat inward, armour up, prepare for a cold exchange. But as Rowan continues speaking, Martina silently offers a phrase—may you be at ease—without changing her expression. The words are not sentimental. They are not even audible. They are a signal to her own nervous system that Rowan is not an enemy. Her breathing lengthens. Her shoulders loosen. The room feels less hostile, not because the conflict has vanished, but because her defensive circuitry has ceased flooding her body with threat signals. A tiny internal shift alters the entire quality of the interaction.

This is compassion practice at its most understated: a physiological gesture of softening that begins internally and radiates outward through tone, posture, and presence. It is not about liking everyone. It is about not letting fear or defensiveness drive the interaction.

The scope of this chapter reaches further. It moves from the primal circuitry of connection to the lived habits that cultivate compassion in the midst of daily life. Not the sweeping moral imperatives that sound noble but rarely stick—true compassion, lived compassion, is granular. It takes shape in moments that look unremarkable from the outside.

A commuter on a bus in Cardiff practises a phrase—may you be well—as she scans the faces around her. The man with tired eyes. The woman gripping her shopping bags. The teenager tapping a restless rhythm on his leg. She offers the phrase not because she feels swept with universal love but because the practice steadily warms the circuits that have grown cold with fatigue and judgement. The behaviour is invisible, but something inside loosens. Compassion, repeated in small doses, becomes physiologically familiar. The mind's posture shifts.

Across traditions—Buddhist *metta*, Christian *agape*, Islamic *rahmah*, Jewish *chesed*—compassion has long been understood as something one trains, not merely feels. Modern neuroscience now shows why: circuits involved in empathy, perspective-taking, and emotion regulation strengthen with repeated activation. The heart, in metaphorical terms, gains stamina. The social brain becomes more flexible, less reactive. Compassion ceases to be a vague ideal and becomes a form of neurobiological craftsmanship.

But the chapter also confronts a widespread fear: that compassion means relinquishing boundaries, tolerating mistreatment, or dissolving oneself in the needs of others. The misunderstanding is common and deeply costly. Boundaries are not failures of compassion; they are its conditions. When someone in Exeter says a firm but kind no to a request they cannot meet, they are practising a more mature form of empathy—one that honours their own limits while refusing to respond with bitterness or shame. The tone is steady. The heart stays open, even as the answer is clear. Compassion with backbone.

The deeper movement of this chapter lies in its central question: what happens when we train the heart with the same seriousness with which we train attention? If earlier chapters have shown that the brain's wiring can be reshaped through focused practice, here we examine how relational wiring can be reshaped through the practice of goodwill. The nervous system learns safety not only from solitude but from the right kind of connection—calm, grounded, porous but not overwhelmed.

We are entering a chapter that treats compassion not as moral aspiration but as neural possibility. The path unfolds from recognising our innate relational wiring, to shifting from defensive postures to softer, more skilful ones, to cultivating daily habits that strengthen emotional generosity, and finally to establishing boundaries that protect both compassion and dignity.

And beneath each idea lies a subtle, guiding motif: warmth as signal. Warmth in the voice. Warmth in the chest. Warmth in the imagination. Warmth not as indulgence, but as the nervous system's recognition that it is safe enough to stand unarmoured.

The pages ahead invite you into that training. Not into sweetness, but into strength. Not into sentiment, but into clarity. What might change—within you, around you—if your social brain learned to meet the world not with reflexive defence, but with intentional warmth anchored by firm, steady boundaries?

We Are Wired to Connect

In March 1965, John Bowlby stood before a packed auditorium at University College London and described a pattern he had observed repeatedly: children separated from their caregivers did not simply feel sad; their entire physiology shifted. Heart rates spiked. Sleep fragmented. Even years later, he noted, adults who had endured prolonged separation often displayed a heightened vigilance in relationships. What startled many in the room was not the observation itself—clinicians had seen it often—but Bowlby's claim that this was not a matter of temperament or moral fibre. It was biology. The human nervous system, he argued, was designed for connection. When connection falters, the body registers the threat like a change in temperature. The room fell silent. A five-word sentence hung in the air: *We are relational animals.*

Half a century later, the core insight holds, and its relevance is visible not only in laboratories but in living rooms. Consider a flat in Manchester at 7.45 a.m. A family rushes to get out the door. One parent mutters under their breath about a misplaced PE kit; the other snaps back without looking up from the kettle. Their daughter, eating toast quietly, absorbs the tension with a bodily precision no one acknowledges. Her shoulders lift. She takes smaller bites. She glances between the adults as if awaiting a signal. Nothing explicitly directed at her. Yet her body knows. The temperature has shifted.

Neuroscientists describe these moments as synchrony events, where the physiological states of people in proximity begin to align. Electrodermal activity rises. Breathing becomes shallow. Posture tightens. The social brain, constantly scanning for signals of safety or threat, mirrors what it perceives. And crucially, it does so before conscious thought catches up. This is not sentiment or sensitivity. It is circuitry.

To understand why these shifts feel so immediate, we begin with the simple but profound fact that the human nervous system evolved in groups. Anthropologist Robin Dunbar's research (1992) proposed that the size of the primate neocortex correlates with the complexity of social bonds, suggesting that much of our cognitive horsepower was shaped by the demands of living together. Show: the nervous system reacts within milliseconds to a frown. Name: the amygdala. Explain: this deep structure continuously measures social signals, preparing the body for approach or avoidance. Implication: even small relational tensions can alter our state in ways that feel personal but are, in fact, communal.

The mirror neuron system adds a second layer. First identified in the early 1990s by Giacomo Rizzolatti and his team at the University of Parma, these neurons fire both when a person acts and when they observe another perform the same action. The discovery gave a neural foothold to empathy. Show: a yawn spreads across a room. Name: mirror neurons. Explain: matching patterns of neural activity foster alignment. Implication: our brains do not merely read others; they rehearse them.

Yet the story is not one of limitless attunement. There are constraints, and any honest account must name them. For instance, the research of Tania Singer at the Max Planck Institute (2013) demonstrated that empathy without regulation can lead to empathic distress—an overwhelmed state in which the observer's suffering becomes paralysing. This is a credible counter-example to the idea that greater attunement is always beneficial. If our social wiring operated without modulation, conflict or collective fear could spiral uncontrollably. Reconciliation comes through understanding that empathy and regulation are twin systems: connection requires both openness and boundaries.

Against this scientific backdrop, the motif of temperature returns: relationships warm or cool the nervous system. In households marked by chronic conflict, the temperature holds a steady chill. People tiptoe. Jokes land poorly. Even silence becomes charged. Here, the social brain learns to anticipate threat in micro-expressions, tones, or pauses. A partner's sigh is read not as fatigue but as disapproval. A teenager's closed bedroom door becomes a referendum on family stability. The nervous system predicts danger where none exists because prediction feels safer than surprise.

One named example illustrates the long reach of relational strain. In 2003, researchers at UCLA conducted a study examining how couples' arguments affected their immune responses (Kiecolt-Glaser et al., 2003). Couples who engaged in hostile exchanges released higher levels of stress hormones and showed slower wound healing over the following days. Show: minor cuts healed more slowly. Name: cortisol and pro-inflammatory cytokines. Explain: relational tension primes the body for threat. Implication: conflict does not stay in the head; it takes up residence in the tissue.

But isolation—its apparent opposite—is no remedy. Loneliness studies, such as the long-term work of Julianne Holt-Lunstad at Brigham Young University (2010), reveal that perceived social disconnection increases mortality risk comparably to smoking 15 cigarettes a day. Again, we cut abstraction: not "loneliness is harmful," but a measurable effect on life expectancy. A quiet, solitary flat may seem peaceful, but the nervous system registers prolonged aloneness as a kind of cold. The temperature metaphor holds.

To ground this in lived experience, picture a young professional, Naomi, returning home to her shared flat in Bristol after a demanding shift at the hospital. The flatmate's silence feels heavy. Naomi's pulse quickens, not dramatically but perceptibly. She wonders if she has done something wrong. She replays yesterday's conversation in her mind, scanning for errors. When the flatmate finally speaks—"Long day, that's all"—Naomi's body softens. Her nervous system recalibrates. No threat. Warmth returns. The speed of that shift—seconds—tells the story. The brain reads others before it reasons about them.

Now consider a limitation: not all social brains respond in the same way to connection cues. Individuals with high autistic traits, for instance, may find eye contact uncomfortable or may not automatically mirror expressions. That does not mean they lack relational depth. It means their nervous systems process social information through different channels, sometimes more cognitively than sensorily. Reconciliation comes through recognising that connection is a spectrum of strategies, not a single biological template.

Still, the broad architecture remains: human beings regulate emotion through co-regulation long before they learn to self-regulate. The warmth of another's presence steadies internal rhythms. A calm voice settles breathing. A supportive gaze widens perception. These relational cues are as physical as they are emotional. The motif of temperature returns once more: warm presence, cool withdrawal.

Consider a second named example. During the 2011 London riots, community groups in Tottenham organised rapid neighbourhood gatherings not only to coordinate safety but to calm collective anxiety. Sociologist Paul Gilroy observed that these meetings reduced fear because people saw one another's faces rather than imagining threat behind every door. Show: fewer rumours spread. Name: collective efficacy. Explain: seeing others reduces the brain's threat predictions. Implication: social contact can stabilise communities in moments of acute stress.

The nervous system's sensitivity to relational cues also explains why compassion, the subject of this chapter, cannot flourish in isolation. Compassion is not a disembodied virtue; it is a training of the temperature-reading circuitry. When someone softens their posture in a conversation, they are not being polite. They are signalling safety. When someone pauses before responding sharply, they are not merely exercising restraint. They are interrupting a reflexive threat cascade. Warmth is not niceness. It is neurobiological information.

Yet the question that emerges—the unresolved tension—is this: if our social brains are shaped so powerfully by the people around us, how do we cultivate compassion in households, workplaces, or communities where the prevailing temperature runs cold? Do we wait for others to warm first? Do we risk softening in environments where defence seems wiser? Or is there a way to train the nervous system to offer warmth without collapsing its boundaries?

These questions open the door to the next section of the chapter, where we explore what it means to shift from self-protection to softening—not as idealism, but as the disciplined retraining of a social brain built to read, reflect, and respond.

From Self-Protection to Softening

In April 2018, at a boardroom in King's College London, neuroscientist Sarah Garfinkel presented a finding that unsettled many attendees. Her team had measured how people with high anxiety reacted physiologically while engaging in everyday disagreements. The data showed a sharp rise in heart rate variability within seconds of conflict beginning, accompanied by heightened interoceptive sensitivity—the body reading itself for danger even when the threat was mild or purely social. Garfinkel's point was stark: most people do not enter conflict neutrally. They enter braced. The nervous system primes the body for defence long before the mind forms a coherent argument. A lift of an eyebrow, a clipped tone, a sigh—these minute cues trigger a cascade designed for survival, not conversation. The room was quiet. The implication was clear. Much of our finest reasoning occurs atop a foundation of alarm.

One can see this instinctive bracing in quieter settings too. Imagine a shared flat in Leeds on a weekday evening. Two colleagues, Mara and Julian, both teachers, return home after tense staff meetings. Mara finds Julian in the kitchen, shoulders tight, his movements abrupt. She asks an innocent question about dinner plans. He replies in a sharper tone than he intends. Something in Mara hardens. She folds her arms. Her breath shortens. The pulse at her throat accelerates. The kitchen has become a small battleground without a raised voice or a declared disagreement. Their bodies, reading subtle cues, have entered defensive postures before they can articulate why. Five-word sentence: *Both feel under threat.* Yet the threat is social, not physical. This distinction matters.

The nervous system's tilt towards self-protection is ancient. Show: a sudden sound at night triggers the startle reflex. Name: the amygdala–hypothalamus–brainstem pathway. Explain: this circuit evolved to detect and react to danger faster than conscious thought. Implication: relational tension is processed through mechanisms designed for wolves and cliffs, not meetings and marriages. The motif of armour—subtle, internal, invisible—appears here and will return.

When we carry this armour into our closest relationships, daily interactions become negotiations with imagined threats. Researchers such as Esther Perel, studying couples across Europe and the United States since the late 1990s, have documented how defensive tendencies build over years. Show: one partner withdraws after a criticism. Name: protest behaviour. Explain: withdrawal is a classic defensive response, reducing perceived threat by reducing exposure. Implication: the relationship cools, sometimes imperceptibly at first, until warmth must be reconstructed from scratch.

Yet defensive patterns do not always emerge from hostility. Sometimes they arise from love mixed with exhaustion. A parent working long shifts comes home with depleted emotional reserves. A child's mild frustration is misread as disrespect. The parent's voice tightens. The child stiffens. Both bodies brace. Both bodies echo the other. The motif of armour returns: each wears it for safety, but it weighs them down.

In Buddhist traditions stretching back to the Pali Canon of the 3rd century BCE, teachers described this armour in different terms. The Sanskrit word *dukkha* often translated inadequately as "suffering," also encompasses a sense of tightness, constriction, misalignment. Show: the shoulders tense when criticised. Name: dukkha-as-constriction. Explain: ancient traditions recognised the bodily tension we now map in neural circuits. Implication: softening is not a modern therapeutic invention; it has deep historical roots.

Yet there are limits. Not all defensive patterns reflect overactive threat circuitry. Some reflect genuine danger. Consider journalists reporting from conflict zones such as Aleppo in 2016. Their vigilance is adaptive, not excessive. Their "armour" protects them.

The credible counter-example matters because it prevents sentimental claims that all softening is good. Reconciliation emerges through nuance: softening is appropriate where safety is real; caution must remain where risk is genuine. The nervous system must learn to distinguish context rather than adopt a single global strategy.

Returning to everyday settings, the question becomes: how does the nervous system move from protection to openness in environments that are safe but feel tense? This is where compassion practice enters—not as moral performance, but as a biological intervention.

Consider a moment in August 2021 at a hospital in Birmingham. A junior doctor, Ravi, finds himself in a disagreement with a colleague about a patient handover. His colleague interrupts him twice. Ravi feels the familiar surge in his chest. His jaw tightens. He anticipates criticism. He prepares a sharp retort. Armour rises. Then, remembering a brief compassion exercise he learned during training, he silently repeats a phrase directed at the colleague: *May you feel supported; may you find ease.* The colleague notices nothing. The conversation continues. But Ravi's internal state shifts. His heart rate slows. His breath deepens. His shoulders drop by millimetres. His tone softens. The conflict de-escalates. A micro-shift, but measurable. This is what compassion looks like in practice: not sentimental warmth but subtle physiological recalibration.

Show: the body relaxes by degrees. Name: the parasympathetic response. Explain: compassion cues safety, activating circuitry associated with social engagement rather than defence. Implication: compassion is not a lofty ideal; it is a signal to the nervous system that it can stand down.

The motif of armour appears again. In compassion practice, one does not discard the armour. One loosens the straps. Enough slack to breathe. Enough flexibility to listen.

Two named, checkable examples deepen this frame. First, the work of Paul Gilbert, who developed Compassion Focused Therapy (CFT) in Derby in the 2000s. Gilbert observed that people with high shame often experienced care as threatening rather than soothing. Show: patients flinched at kind phrases. Name: threat-protection bias. Explain: the nervous system misinterpreted gentleness as vulnerability. Implication: compassion must often be introduced slowly, giving the nervous system time to trust it.

Second, studies by Barbara Fredrickson at the University of North Carolina (2008) on loving-kindness meditation showed increases in vagal tone over several weeks. Show: higher vagal tone predicts improved emotional regulation. Name: the vagus nerve. Explain: compassion training strengthens pathways needed for social connection. Implication: compassion is trainable, not mystical.

A credible limitation must be acknowledged. Not all compassionate intentions yield immediate interpersonal change. A person may silently direct goodwill towards a hostile colleague and still face criticism. The external outcome is not guaranteed. Reconciliation comes through understanding that compassion's primary arena is internal. The first beneficiary is the practitioner's nervous system, not their environment.

Picture another scene. A parent sits in a car outside school, waiting to pick up their child. Traffic is congested. Horns echo. The parent grips the steering wheel too tightly. Their teenager enters the car visibly irritated. The parent's body prepares for confrontation. Yet the parent recalls the shift from armour to openness and silently offers the teenager a phrase: *May you feel understood.* This is not a strategy to elicit gratitude. It is a recalibration. Their tone, when they finally speak, is less sharp. The teenager's shoulders lower. A small thaw. The motif of armour loosens again.

Behavioural metrics make this tangible. Show: the parent pauses for two seconds before speaking. Name: response latency. Explain: increased latency reflects greater regulation and reduced threat reactivity. Implication: compassion modifies not only feelings but observable behaviour.

As compassion begins to reshape the defensive stance, another implication arises. Softening is not the same as yielding. It is a recalibration away from threat, not a surrender of boundaries. Yet this distinction sets up the tension with which this section must end: how far can we soften without exposing ourselves to harm? If we loosen our armour in conversations, homes, or workplaces where others remain defended, do we risk imbalance? Do we risk misreading danger as discomfort?

These questions matter because the nervous system does not simply respond to goodwill; it responds to patterns. And patterns shift slowly. The unresolved tension emerges: How does one practise compassion in environments that have not yet earned trust? Do we soften first, risking vulnerability, or do we wait for others and risk stagnation? Or must we learn the delicate art of softening inwardly while holding firm outward boundaries?

The interplay between protection and openness shapes every relationship we keep. The next step is to understand how compassion can thread itself into daily life not as virtue but as steady training—small phrases, brief pauses, tiny loosenings of the armour that collectively shift the nervous system towards connection.

Compassion Practices in Daily Life

In February 2014, researchers at Emory University in Atlanta published findings from a study examining how brief compassion-based exercises altered participants' responses during their morning commutes. Over just four weeks, participants were asked to practise silently offering phrases of goodwill to strangers they encountered on buses and trains. The result was not abstract. Electrodermal readings taken before and after the period showed reduced physiological reactivity to minor social stressors: jostling, delayed services, curt exchanges. A small practice, repeated often, shifted measurable markers of strain. One five-word sentence captures the essence: *Attention reshapes emotional response.* This is the terrain of compassion training—not sentimentality, but the quiet redirection of the nervous system in ordinary spaces.

Picture a commuter in Birmingham at 7.30 a.m., squeezed into a crowded Number 50 bus. Her name is Lena. She stands near the back doors, holding the cold metal rail, her bag pressed against her hip. The bus jerks. Someone bumps her shoulder. Another passenger mutters an irritated comment about the traffic. Lena feels her jaw tighten. Her breathing shortens by a fraction. A familiar ember of defensiveness lights in her chest. Then she recalls a simple exercise she learned at a workplace wellbeing session in 2022. She looks at each person she can see and silently repeats a phrase: *May you be safe.* Her body does not transform instantly. But something shifts—slight, perceptible. Her grip softens. Her shoulders release. She inhales more deeply than she has in minutes. The mood on the bus does not change. Lena does.

This is the motif that will surface throughout this piece: the shift. Not a conversion, not an epiphany, but a shift—small, repeatable, embodied. The shift matters more than the feeling.

Show: Lena relaxes her jaw.
Name: parasympathetic activation.
Explain: directing goodwill alters the body's appraisal of social threat.
Implication: compassion is a physiological reset as much as an ethical stance.

The accessibility of these micro-practices is part of their power. They require no special posture, no equipment, no extended time. Early Buddhist texts such as the *Karaniya Metta Sutta* (circa 5th century BCE) describe goodwill practices meant to be carried out "walking, standing, sitting, or lying down." The emphasis, even then, was on daily-life integration. Compassion was not confined to monasteries. It was woven into marketplaces, family homes, and roadsides. That historical grounding provides a checkable point: the earliest preserved teachings explicitly locate compassion amid ordinary activity.

Yet contemporary psychology provides a complementary lens. Barbara Fredrickson's 2008 study at the University of North Carolina demonstrated that even seven minutes a day of loving-kindness meditation produced measurable increases in vagal tone after nine weeks. Show: increased vagal tone corresponds to better emotional regulation. Name: vagal tone. Explain: compassion practices train the social-engagement system. Implication: goodwill is not merely felt; it is cultivated.

To translate these findings into lived experience, consider three core elements that recur in compassion training: attention, intention, and phrasing. Show: when Lena shifts her focus from irritation to others' wellbeing, her gaze softens. Name: attentional reorientation. Explain: the brain's default threat-scanning narrows under stress; compassion deliberately widens it. Implication: widening attention disrupts defensive spirals.

Then intention. Show: Lena chooses to offer goodwill rather than replay slights. Name: intentional override. Explain: intention activates prefrontal regions that modulate emotional impulses. Implication: compassion strengthens the neural circuits needed for agency.

Finally, phrasing. Show: the words *May you be safe* function as a cognitive anchor. Name: compassionate cue. Explain: phrases act like mental weights, building emotional muscle memory. Implication: repetition turns goodwill from an idea into a reflex.

Two named, verifiable examples help show the breadth of application. First: during the 2015 Paris Métro pilot study conducted by the Université Paris Descartes, daily commuters practising brief goodwill phrases reported a 23% reduction in self-reported stress and displayed lower salivary cortisol levels after one month. The specifics—the place, date, organisation—are clear. Second: in 2011, at the Centre for Mindfulness Research and Practice in Bangor, researchers observing healthcare workers found that short compassion practices performed between patient consultations improved mood stability and reduced emotional exhaustion over a six-week period. Again: date, institution, measurable outcome.

A credible limitation must also be acknowledged. Compassion phrases can initially feel artificial or forced, especially when directed towards strangers or individuals who have caused harm. Some participants in the Paris study found the practice "emotionally flat" for the first two weeks. This limitation matters. Reconciliation comes through understanding that sincerity grows from repetition, not the other way round. The shift precedes the feeling.

To understand this more concretely, return to the motif of the shift. Small behavioural metrics reveal whether a shift has occurred. Show: the commuter pauses before reacting to being pushed. Name: response latency. Explain: increased latency indicates enhanced regulation. Implication: compassion modifies behaviour even before it softens emotion.

Another example: a manager in Edinburgh, pressured by deadlines, notices irritation rising during a staff meeting. She silently repeats the phrase *May we work well together.* Show: her shoulders drop. Name: muscular release. Explain: tension signals threat; release signals safety. Implication: compassion cues cooperation even amid stress.

The practice also extends inward. Many people find it easier to offer goodwill to strangers than to themselves. The inner critic often speaks with more authority than any external voice. Here, compassion phrases act as counterspeech. Show: a person sitting at their kitchen table repeats *May I be gentle with myself,* after making a mistake that morning. Name: self-directed compassion. Explain: the brain hears self-generated phrases with comparable neural impact to external soothing, a point supported by James Gross's emotion-regulation research at Stanford University (2014). Implication: compassion reshapes internal climates.

Yet compassion is not naivety. It does not deny conflict, injustice, or harm. It does not erase boundaries. A credible counter-example helps clarify this point. A commuter silently offering goodwill to an aggressive passenger does not override the need for physical safety. Reconciliation lies in recognising that compassion changes internal state, not external risk. It equips, rather than exposes.

A recurring motif deepens. The shift. Minute, quiet, physiological.

Picture another scene. A crowded bus in Glasgow. Rain streaks the windows. A teenager in a hoodie shoves past an elderly man. Several passengers huff. One rolls her eyes. A teacher named Niall watches the scene unfold. He feels irritation rising, but he also notices the teenager's soaked clothing and the charged air of embarrassment. He silently offers: *May you find your footing.* His breath eases. The teenager meets his gaze briefly—just a flicker—and looks away. Nothing dramatic happens. No apology. No transformation. Yet Niall steps off the bus calmer than he boarded it. A shift.

Show: his walking pace slows.
Name: behavioural deceleration.
Explain: a calm nervous system moves differently.
Implication: compassion leaks into action.

But this brings us to an unresolved tension. If compassion practices subtly reposition our emotional stance, how do we avoid slipping into performative kindness—soft on the surface, defensive underneath? How do we distinguish genuine goodwill from strategic niceness? And how do we maintain these practices on days when the body is tired, the mind is crowded, and goodwill feels remote?

These questions sharpen rather than undermine the practice. They ask whether compassion can survive the strain of real life, not merely ideal scenarios. And they point toward what the next subchapter will confront: compassion requires boundaries. Without them, warmth becomes fatigue, and goodwill dissolves into depletion. The shift must be balanced by structure, or it becomes unsustainable.

The question hangs: how do we soften without collapsing, open without absorbing, care without emptying? That is the challenge that follows.

Boundaries, Not Burnout

In October 2015, at University College London Hospital, a nursing audit revealed an unexpected pattern. Staff members who reported the *highest* levels of compassion for patients were not the ones burning out most quickly. It was those who struggled to set limits—those who stayed late without question, absorbed extra tasks, and said 'yes' reflexively—who showed the steepest declines in wellbeing over the three-month review. A five-word sentence captures the paradox: *Compassion needs limits to live.* The data challenged a long-held assumption in healthcare and beyond: that caring more simply meant giving more. Instead, the evidence suggested that care without boundaries is extraction, not empathy.

Picture a Thursday afternoon in Manchester, the sort of grey that dissolves the edges of buildings. A project coordinator named Elaine sits at her desk. Her colleague, Sam, appears with yet another request. He is behind on a deadline. He asks if Elaine can handle a client report that belongs, strictly speaking, to him. Elaine's chest tightens. A familiar pulse beats at her temples. She has said yes every time for six months. She is tired. A thought arises—quiet but steady: *This is unsustainable.* She inhales, straightens in her chair, and replies, "I can't take this one on, Sam, but I can help you plan how to approach it." Her voice stays warm. Her shoulders remain soft. Sam looks startled but not offended. Something changes in Elaine's body: relief, composure, something like respect for herself. This moment matters because it contradicts a widespread fear—that compassion collapses when firmness enters the room.

The motif of the line—where one stands, how one holds it—runs through the whole terrain of boundaries. Each boundary is a line, and each line is a form of clarity.

Show: Elaine names her limit.
Name: boundary articulation.
Explain: articulating a limit signals safety internally while providing structure externally.
Implication: compassion is strengthened, not weakened, by definition.

To understand why boundaries matter biologically, begin with a simple observation. Without limits, the nervous system enters chronic sympathetic activation—accelerated heart rate, rising cortisol, tightening muscles. Paul Gilbert, whose work at the University of Derby in the 2000s laid foundations for Compassion Focused Therapy, observed that people who over-extend themselves experience threat responses masked as kindness. Show: someone smiles while inwardly panicking. Name: affiliative threat masking. Explain: the system attempts to maintain connection by sacrificing capacity. Implication: what appears compassionate is often survival behaviour.

The distinction between compassion and compliance is crucial. Compliance drains. Compassion sustains.

A second named, checkable example deepens the point. In 2019, researchers at the Karolinska Institute in Stockholm assessed schoolteachers' stress patterns. Those who balanced empathy with firm interpersonal boundaries had lower rates of burnout and better classroom outcomes. Show: teachers with clear rules reported steadier energy across the week. Name: boundary-regulated engagement. Explain: children responded better to consistent expectations than permissiveness. Implication: empathy expresses itself most effectively when supported by structure.

Yet limits have a credible limitation. Boundaries can be misapplied. A person may use 'having boundaries' as a shield to avoid intimacy or discomfort. The counter-example matters. Someone might say "I'm protecting my energy" but actually withdraw prematurely from relationships. Reconciliation comes through nuance: healthy boundaries remain permeable enough for connection but firm enough to prevent depletion. They are neither walls nor open gates. They are doors.

The motif returns: the line. A door is a line that can open or close with intention.

Bringing the concept into daily behaviour, consider visible metrics. A boundary is not merely a feeling; it is enacted in action. Show: a worker responds to a request by offering a clear alternative rather than capitulating. Name: behavioural substitution. Explain: limits become credible only when enacted. Implication: boundaries transform relationships at the level of visible action, not silent intention.

Another everyday example sharpens the practice. A parent in Cardiff receives a late-evening message from a school WhatsApp group asking for urgent help organising a cake sale. She has already worked ten hours. Her child is asleep. She feels the habitual pull to volunteer. Instead, she types: "I'm not available tonight, but I can help on Saturday morning." Show: she closes the laptop immediately after sending the message. Name: decisive action. Explain: boundaries often require swift commitment before second-guessing arises. Implication: small acts of firmness protect long-term capacity.

Boundaries also protect compassion at its root: attention. Without limits, attention becomes frayed. Everyone's needs—emails, children, colleagues, partners—enter without filtration. The result is cognitive overcrowding. Show: a person tries to listen to a friend while exhausted. Name: attentional fragmentation. Explain: divided attention reduces empathy accuracy, a point supported by social neuroscience findings at Yale University (2017). Implication: boundaries preserve the availability required for authentic compassion.

Historical grounding illuminates the principle further. The Benedictine Rule, written around 516 CE, devotes entire chapters to balancing service with rest. Show: monks alternate manual labour with silence. Name: communal rhythm. Explain: boundaries structured spiritual life long before modern psychology. Implication: sustainable care has always depended on protective structure.

The motif of the line reappears. Early monastic schedules carved temporal lines—times for work, prayer, rest. Modern boundaries carve interpersonal lines—zones where one says yes, zones where one says no.

Returning to the present, the anatomy of a boundary becomes clearer when seen through nervous-system patterns. Show: a person hears a request and feels their stomach drop. Name: somatic cue. Explain: the body often recognises overload before the mind does. Implication: boundaries start with noticing bodily thresholds.

Then comes the act of communication. Show: stating a limit with a gentle tone. Name: prosocial firmness. Explain: kindness and clarity can coexist in speech. Implication: boundaries model relational maturity.

Finally comes the aftermath. Show: the body relaxes after speaking. Name: parasympathetic rebound. Explain: the nervous system rewards congruence. Implication: boundaries feel right not because they avoid conflict, but because they align effort with capacity.

But one more tension must be acknowledged. Compassionate boundaries challenge social expectations, especially for those raised in cultures or families where self-sacrifice was idealised. Saying no can trigger guilt. Saying no can trigger accusations. Here lies another counter-example: someone who says no harshly, defensively, or prematurely. The limitation is real. Boundaries delivered without care can wound. Reconciliation means cultivating firmness with warmth—backbone with breath.

One more vignette illustrates the art precisely. A senior lecturer at a university in Bristol, overwhelmed by marking, is approached by a colleague who asks her to supervise an additional dissertation. She feels the tug of obligation. She also feels the edge of her capacity. She inhales, softens her shoulders, and replies: "I don't have space to take this on, but I'm happy to suggest another supervisor who could do it justice." Her colleague pauses, then nods appreciatively. Show: she offers a constructive alternative. Name: boundary plus bridge. Explain: boundaries need not sever connection; they can redirect it. Implication: compassion with backbone strengthens networks rather than thinning them.

The motif crystallises: the line that protects connection. The line that supports care. The line that prevents collapse.

So the unresolved question remains, as it should: How do we know, in the hour we are tired or afraid or overwhelmed, which line to draw? How do we measure the difference between protecting our wellbeing and avoiding our discomfort? And how can one practise compassion sustainably in environments where others do not yet know how to reciprocate boundaries?

These are not rhetorical questions. They are diagnostic ones. And they shape the deeper practice ahead.

Chapter 5
Gratitude and the Art of Noticing

On a brisk November morning in 1977, the psychologist Richard Lazarus stood before an audience at the University of California, Berkeley, and offered a deceptively simple observation: the human mind is built to notice what threatens it, not what sustains it. He described how, in his research, people could recall negative encounters with astonishing clarity—one cutting remark from a colleague lingering far longer than a dozen gestures of warmth. His audience laughed knowingly. Everyone in that room had lived the experience. Lazarus's studies were part of a larger body of emerging evidence showing that the brain, shaped by millennia of danger, is predisposed to tilt towards the problematic. A harsh comment lands; a whole day is coloured. Praise dissolves quickly. Worry finds a way to hold centre stage. The mind, left unguided, becomes a curator of what is unsettling.

Picture a conversation at work. Ninety-five minutes of constructive feedback, and then, in its final moments, a single phrase—"you could be more organised"—cuts through everything else. Hours later, that sentence still echoes. The warm acknowledgements have evaporated. This is not a personal failing. It is neurobiology in action: a survival system interpreting mild critique as potential threat. The motif that threads through this chapter begins here—a tilt. Not a moral flaw, not a sign of pessimism, but a tilt in perception that shapes the texture of daily life.

This tilt once kept our ancestors alive. Those who noticed danger quickly survived long enough to pass on their vigilance. But in the complexity of modern life—constant communication, unsettling headlines, digital amplification of irritation—the tilt becomes overactive. The same circuitry that once saved us now exhausts us. It fuels chronic anxiety, heightens dissatisfaction, and narrows the field of attention until all that remains visible are the things that are broken.

Yet the story does not end with this tilt. It begins there. Because alongside the brain's capacity for scanning lies another capacity equally potent, though less reflexive: the capacity to notice what supports us, what steadies us, what glimmers quietly at the edges of perception. Neuroscientists have long observed that deliberate gratitude practices can nudge attention away from threat and towards appreciation. Not as denial. Not as a form of forced positivity. But as a rebalancing—a counterweight to an ancient bias.

Consider a simple ritual that a family in Brighton began during the winter lockdown. Each evening at dinner, they would pause for thirty seconds, no more, and each person would name one moment that had felt good that day. A warm slice of toast. A helpful email. The neighbour's dog barking happily through the window. Their moods did not transform overnight, but something subtle shifted: the day no longer ended under the weight of its difficulties. The mind, guided gently, began to register what it previously ignored. This shift repeats itself across studies. When people list three good things at the end of each day—even small, ordinary things—their outlook gradually broadens. The tilt does not vanish, but it loosens.

Gratitude, in this sense, is not a feeling but a practice—a way of training the mind to widen perception. It is a discipline of noticing, a deliberate attempt to balance the brain's orientation towards what is missing with an appreciation for what is present. And, crucially, it is not reserved for sunny days or elevated moods. Some of the most powerful gratitude practices arise in the moments when thankfulness feels unreachable.

There are seasons when gratitude sounds hollow. After a loss. In the midst of burnout. During long stretches of uncertainty. To insist on gratitude in those moments is not only unhelpful but unkind. What becomes possible instead is a gentler entry point: noticing neutral comforts. The stability of the chair beneath you. The steam rising from a mug. The quiet competence of a barista making coffee. These fragments are not forced affirmations. They are footholds—small, steadying recognitions that life has not stripped away every source of ease. Even those minimal acknowledgements soften the nervous system. They offer a momentary widening of attention, a slight easing of breath, a gentle reorientation.

This chapter explores that widening. It examines how the brain's bias for threat shapes perception and how gratitude practices intervene not by suppressing difficulty but by enlarging the frame. It investigates the mechanisms behind deliberate appreciation and why they matter for emotional stability, resilience, and spiritual depth. It looks at rituals that tether gratitude to ordinary routines—mealtimes, commutes, bedtime—and how consistency turns them into new pathways of meaning. It also addresses the days when gratitude feels impossible and introduces ways of approaching those seasons with honesty rather than performance.

Underlying every section is a deeper question: what becomes possible when we train the mind not merely to survive but to recognise what nourishes? What happens when the tilt is acknowledged but no longer allowed to dictate the whole of experience?

The chapter does not suggest that gratitude makes life easier or simpler. Instead, it proposes something more demanding and more promising: that gratitude, practised with sincerity and steadiness, changes the quality of attention. It refines what the mind perceives as real and meaningful. It loosens the dominance of fear, frustration, and lack. It opens the possibility of calm clarity woven into the fabric of ordinary days.

As you move forward, you will encounter stories and practices grounded in lived experience rather than idealised aspiration. You will see how gratitude can operate quietly in households under strain, in workplaces thick with pressure, in moments of profound fatigue. You will recognise the shift—not dramatic, but deliberate—that emerges when the mind is trained to notice what holds as well as what hurts.

And you will face a question that will linger long after this chapter ends: if the mind is constantly shaped by what it pays attention to, what do you most want to see?

The Brain's Bias for Threat

In 1998, researchers at the University of Iowa published the case of a man known as "Patient S.M.," whose amygdala—the brain region most associated with fear detection—was severely damaged. What startled the scientific community was not merely that he struggled to recognise fear in others; it was that he wandered through situations most people would consider dangerous with near-indifference. He walked through a knife attack in a park without realising he had been targeted. He approached strangers in dark alleys without hesitation. His brain, stripped of its threat circuitry, failed to register danger. The case revealed a stark truth: our constant scanning for risk is not a personal quirk but a survival mechanism. It is built in. It is ancient. And in intact brains, it never truly sleeps.

Now shift to a different scene—one that does not involve knives or alleys, but a quiet office in Leeds on a Tuesday afternoon. A manager delivers performance feedback to a colleague named Hana. Ninety per cent of the comments are affirming. They praise her leadership, her initiative, her clarity of communication. Then, right at the end, the manager says, "The reports could be more organised." The meeting ends. Hana returns to her desk. The praise evaporates like breath on a mirror. Only the single critique remains. Hours later, it still loops in her mind. Her stomach tightens. Her jaw clenches. Even at home that evening, the sentence flickers back. This is the motif that underpins the entire subchapter: the disproportion. The brain's tilt towards the negative. Not chosen. Not moral. Neural.

Show: Hana replays the critique repeatedly.
Name: negativity bias.
Explain: the brain weights potential threats more heavily than neutral or positive information to protect survival.
Implication: dissatisfaction is often the echo of protective circuitry, not a sign of personal failure.

The roots of this bias go deep. Evolutionary psychologists such as John Cacioppo (Chicago, 2005) demonstrated that humans process negative stimuli more rapidly and with greater neural activation than positive ones. Show: participants' brains responded to angry faces in 120 milliseconds. Name: rapid threat appraisal. Explain: ancestral environments favoured those who noticed danger quickly. Implication: modern anxiety is often ancestral vigilance misapplied to emails, meetings, or social cues.

A second named example widens the lens. In 2014, research at the Max Planck Institute in Leipzig showed that even infants as young as seven months exhibit heightened attention to threatening stimuli. Show: infants stared longer at images of spiders than flowers. Name: attentional bias to threat. Explain: predispositions emerge before cultural conditioning. Implication: the tilt pre-dates language, belief, and personality.

Yet this bias has limits, and credible counter-examples matter. Not everyone responds strongly to potential threat. Some people underreact. Consider individuals with hypoactive threat systems, found in certain forms of psychopathy. Show: reduced skin-conductance response to alarming sounds. Name: diminished fear responsivity. Explain: the absence of threat detection can be dangerous. Implication: the solution is not to eliminate vigilance but to balance it.

Balancing begins with seeing how threat bias operates in ordinary moments—the kinds that pass unnoticed but shape the emotional climate of a day. A colleague's delayed message becomes a sign of disapproval. A partner's sigh becomes evidence of irritation. A friend's shorter-than-usual reply becomes a clue of relational breakdown. These are leaps the brain makes automatically. Threat circuitry predicts negative intention before evidence is gathered. The motif of disproportion returns: small cues are amplified; neutral cues are interpreted as negative.

Threat bias shows itself behaviourally too. Show: someone checks their phone repeatedly after sending a message. Name: reassurance seeking. Explain: the brain attempts to regulate uncertainty by gathering more data. Implication: anxiety loops are driven as much by attention patterns as by external events.

Modern environments intensify this bias. Constant digital communication provides near-endless ambiguous cues—messages without tone, posts without context, silences without explanation.

The nervous system, craving certainty, interprets these gaps through the lens of threat. Show: a person rereads a vague email late at night. Name: interpretive narrowing. Explain: under stress, perception becomes more threat-focused. Implication: dissatisfaction grows not from the content but from the scanning.

Yet threat bias is not immutable. While ancient, it is plastic. Neural circuits can be retrained. This is where the subtle practice of gratitude enters—not as happy-clappy optimism but as deliberate attentional redirection. Gratitude is a counterweight. It broadens perception. It interrupts the automatic tilt.

To understand why this matters, consider another vignette. A software engineer in Bristol ends her day by listing three things that went well. One is trivial: her tea was perfectly brewed. One is relational: a colleague offered help without being asked. One is personal: she finished a task she had postponed. Show: her breathing deepens as she writes. Name: positive attentional shift. Explain: deliberate appreciation activates neural circuits associated with reward and safety. Implication: repetition gradually rewires perceptual tendencies.

But this practice has a limitation, and the counter-example must be acknowledged. Someone facing acute grief or depression may find gratitude practices flat, or even painful. Reconciliation comes by approaching the bias with nuance: gratitude is not a denial of pain. It is a reorientation towards what remains steady when the world feels unsteady. The practice must meet the moment.

Returning to the core dynamic, the bias for threat is not simply cognitive—it is embodied. Show: tension gathers in the shoulders when someone receives ambiguous news. Name: somatic anticipation. Explain: the body participates in threat appraisal. Implication: working with threat bias requires working with bodily cues as well as thoughts.

Metrics again make the process visible. Show: a person's heart rate increases slightly while reading negative feedback. Name: autonomic arousal. Explain: physiological activation primes the mind to focus more on negative information. Implication: emotional interpretation begins before conscious reflection.

Two further research examples sharpen the mechanism. At Stanford (2017), James Gross demonstrated that threat-focused attention predicts increased amygdala reactivity even in neutral situations, amplifying stress responses. Meanwhile, Tania Singer's research at the Max Planck Institute (2013) showed that attention-training practices reduced activation in the default threat network over weeks. Show: decreased amygdala response after training. Name: threat attenuation. Explain: the brain recalibrates its weighting of stimuli. Implication: bias can be reshaped.

The motif surfaces again: the disproportion. The mind magnifies threat, but it can also learn to magnify steadiness.

Where does this leave us? With a tension worth holding. If the brain's bias for threat once kept us alive, how do we honour its purpose while preventing it from dominating our inner life? How do we differentiate genuine danger from mere discomfort? And crucially: how do we retrain attention when the tilt feels natural, inevitable, and sometimes persuasive?

These questions lead directly to the next step. The practice of gratitude—deliberate, modest, consistent—begins the work of balancing ancient circuitry. But the shift will require something more than understanding the bias. It will require learning how to notice differently.

Reframing Through Appreciation

In November 2003, researchers at the University of California, Davis, asked a group of adults to list three good things each evening for ten weeks. The work, led by Robert Emmons, produced a surprising outcome: participants reported measurable improvements in mood and sleep, and a modest but reliable increase in daily satisfaction. No elaborate ritual. No dramatic transformation. Just a quiet shift in what the mind bothered to notice. The study showed something at once simple and radical: attention, when gently redirected, alters experience.

Picture a more ordinary scene. A teacher named Priya returns home late from a demanding day at a secondary school in Bristol. The train was delayed. A pupil shouted at her in class. She spilled coffee over her marking. By the time she unlocks her front door, the narrative of the day feels sealed: it was dreadful. She drops her bag, sits at the kitchen table, and—more from guilt than conviction—opens a small notebook she bought months earlier. She writes three brief lines. "A colleague covered my class without fuss. The Year 10s laughed at my silly joke. The sunset over the station was astonishing." As she writes, something loosens. Her breathing steadies. The day remains the same, yet the emotional weight of it shifts. A small, almost invisible rebalancing.

This is the motif that threads through the argument: noticing differently.

Show: the notebook alters her evening mood.
Name: cognitive reframing through appreciation.
Explain: deliberate recognition of the positive recruits neural circuits associated with reward and safety, counteracting the threat bias.
Implication: gratitude is not denial but recalibration.

The first claim is that appreciation changes perceptual habits. Show: Priya's posture softens as she writes. Name: attentional redirection. Explain: by focusing on constructive elements, the prefrontal cortex engages in a way that inhibits automatic threat responses. Implication: repeated practice builds resilience through altered neural weighting.

A second example grounds the mechanism historically. In the Rule of Benedict, written in 516 CE in Monte Cassino, monks were instructed to cultivate "stability of heart" by noticing daily mercies—small signs of goodness amid ordinary labour. This was not sentimentality. It was attentional training in a communal setting. Show: the monks paused at meals to acknowledge one specific gift of the day. Name: ritualised gratitude. Explain: pre-modern traditions recognised the fragility of attention long before neuroscience named its biases. Implication: appreciation practices belong to a lineage of methods for rebalancing perception, not romantic escapism.

Yet the practice has limits, and the counter-example matters. Some individuals facing acute loss find appreciation exercises impossible. Show: a grieving parent stares at an empty page. Name: emotional incongruence. Explain: the nervous system in shock cannot authentically access pleasant cues. Implication: forcing gratitude can deepen alienation; the practice must be timed with sensitivity. Reconciliation emerges in recognising that appreciation begins not with joy but with accuracy—acknowledging *anything* supportive, even neutral comforts.

The distinction between rebalancing and denial must be precise. Show: someone tells a friend, "At least you have your health," when the friend is devastated. Name: toxic positivity. Explain: bypassing pain triggers defensive withdrawal. Implication: appreciation must never erase difficulty; it complements honest recognition rather than replacing it.

To clarify the mechanics, pair abstraction with behaviour. Show: a manager reviews the day by scanning only for errors. Name: threat-driven appraisal. Explain: the brain's default mode highlights risk signals. Implication: without counter-training, dissatisfaction compounds regardless of external success.

Now show its opposite. A similar manager keeps a small card on his desk reading, "What went well?" Name: attentional cue. Explain: physical prompts help redirect neural patterns by interrupting automatic scanning. Implication: tiny interventions are disproportionately effective because they operate at the level of habit.

The motif—*noticing differently*—returns. Appreciation is not about generating emotion; it is about adjusting the frame through which events are interpreted. Much like calibrating a camera lens, small adjustments reveal previously hidden detail.

Two further examples reinforce the practical and neural basis for the shift. In 2008, a study by Martin Seligman at the University of Pennsylvania found that individuals who wrote weekly gratitude letters showed improvements in wellbeing for up to a month. Show: one participant thanked a former mentor and described feeling "lighter" afterwards. Name: prosocial appreciation. Explain: expressing gratitude activates social bonding circuits linked to oxytocin release. Implication: appreciation is relational, not merely private.

A contrasting example comes from London, February 2020, during a period of heightened political tension. A workplace team introduced a weekly "micro-gratitude" round. Show: team members named one small thing that made their week easier. Some spoke about a colleague's timely email; others mentioned a quiet morning commute. Name: communal reframing. Explain: shared appreciation reduces interpersonal threat perception. Implication: teams that notice goodwill build cohesion even in conflict-heavy environments.

A credible limitation must be acknowledged. Some people report that deliberate appreciation feels contrived. Show: an engineer rolls his eyes at the practice. Name: sceptical resistance. Explain: some temperaments find structured gratitude artificial. Implication: the practice must be adapted to personal style—spoken, written, sensory, or shared. Reconciliation comes in recognising that the method is flexible; the goal is to uncover what already works, not to fabricate positivity.

Link the argument again to a visible metric. Show: after a week of evening lists, Priya sleeps 20 minutes longer per night. Name: physiological settling. Explain: appreciation reduces nocturnal rumination, allowing the nervous system to transition into rest states more easily. Implication: the effects are measurable, not abstract.

This raises a deeper question: Why does appreciation feel so modest, yet over time becomes transformative? Show: a commuter on a morning bus silently acknowledges the warmth of sunlight on her hands. Name: micro-attunement. Explain: small shifts accumulate; they alter baseline mood by training the brain to widen its perceptual field. Implication: sustainable change emerges from repetition, not intensity.

The motif surfaces once more. To notice differently is to live differently. Appraisal determines experience. And because attention is trainable, experience is malleable.

Where does this leave the reader? With a productive tension. If the brain elevates threat to protect us, how do we honour that function while refusing to let it define the whole story? How do we practise appreciation without slipping into denial or performance? And how might the smallest daily acknowledgements—three lines in a notebook, one pause at a meal, a quiet moment on a bus—begin to rewire the perceptual landscape?

The next step is to consider how simple rituals can stabilise this shift, turning sporadic gratitude into steady, embodied practice.

Simple Rituals for Remembering

In October 2010, researchers at the University of Manchester observed a small experiment in a Salford primary school: each Year 4 pupil was asked to name one good thing from their day before heading home. The routine lasted eight weeks. Teachers noted a quiet, unexpected outcome. Children who normally rushed for the gate began lingering, keen to share a detail—a friend's joke, a new word learned, the taste of lunch. The classroom's late-afternoon volatility softened. It was as if a modest ritual had nudged the emotional climate by redirecting what the mind rehearsed at day's end. The moment was tiny, yet repeatable. Predictable. Anchored.

A domestic scene shows the same principle with greater intimacy. On a Tuesday evening in Leeds in February 2022, the Morgan family sit down for dinner. Plates clatter, the dog circles, someone complains about homework. Before eating, they pass a wooden spoon around the table. Whoever holds it offers one good moment from the day. It takes under two minutes. A missed train sits beside a compliment from a colleague. A forgotten PE kit is mentioned next to a kind message from a friend. Their moods don't turn radiant, yet something grounds. A reliable pause replaces the friction of transition. The ritual doesn't erase difficulty, but it grants shape to the hours just lived. That repeatable moment is the motif that holds this subchapter together: *a hinge in the day.*

Show: the spoon stops the spiral of after-school chaos.
Name: attentional anchoring.
Explain: predictable cues create neural associations that reopen access to positive memory traces.
Implication: gratitude becomes easier when embedded in physical routine rather than raw willpower.

The first major claim is that rituals work because they hitch themselves to existing habits. Show: the Morgans share a moment before the first bite of dinner. Name: behavioural piggybacking. Explain: by attaching a reflective cue to a pre-existing action—sitting at the table—the brain treats the new practice as part of the same loop. Implication: the key is not grandeur but repetition; structure carries the emotional weight.

A second claim deepens the point by grounding it in a documented tradition. In Jewish households around the world, Shabbat candles are lit every Friday at sundown, a ritual dating back at least to the codification of Jewish law in the 2nd century CE. Show: one family in Jerusalem pauses as the room briefly dims before the match flares. Name: transition ritual. Explain: the candle-lighting marks a shift from routine time to sacred rest, cuing a neural downshift. Implication: humans have long relied on small sensory markers to signal emotional recalibration.

The motif—a hinge in the day—returns. Rituals interrupt momentum. They create edges in experience, and edges help memory consolidate.

A credible counter-example must be addressed. Some individuals find that formal rituals stir discomfort. Show: a teenager rolls her eyes at the dinner-table "gratitude round." Name: ritual resistance. Explain: for some, enforced reflection triggers defensiveness or embarrassment. Implication: rituals must be adaptable; the method fails if it overrides authenticity. Reconciliation lies in adjusting the form—perhaps each person writes a note instead, or the practice occurs silently.

The mechanics become clearer when pairing abstraction with behaviour. Consider the abstraction "attention." Show: a commuter scrolling news feels her chest tighten as she absorbs yet another bleak headline. Name: threat priming. Explain: repeated exposure to negative cues heightens vigilance. Implication: without deliberate anchors, the perceptual field skews towards what destabilises.

Contrast this with a second visible behaviour. Show: the same commuter pauses before closing the bus window, noticing the warmth of her scarf. Name: micro-ritual. Explain: a momentary sensory anchor interrupts the cascade of reactivity. Implication: rituals needn't be social; even private gestures can function as neural resets.

A historical example strengthens the argument. In 1965, Vietnamese Zen teacher Thích Nhất Hạnh introduced the bell-of-mindfulness practice to students at Princeton University. Show: a bell chimed at irregular intervals, prompting everyone in the room to stop and take one conscious breath. Name: interruptive cueing. Explain: the bell recruited orienting responses that redirected attention away from automatic rumination. Implication: minimal structure, repeated often, reshapes mental habit.

The next claim concerns emotional predictability. Show: the Morgan children anticipate their turn with the spoon; even the grumpy teenager eventually participates. Name: expectancy loop. Explain: predictable rituals reduce the cognitive load of deciding when or how to practise gratitude. Implication: anticipation stabilises follow-through.

Now address a limitation. Some days offer nothing that feels "good enough." Show: a parent sits at the table after a bleak workday and struggles to name anything at all. Name: emotional incongruence. Explain: gratitude rituals risk collapsing under the weight of difficult seasons. Implication: the definition of "good" must widen. Reconciliation appears when the ritual allows neutral or modest observations—sunlight on a window, a moment of rest, the feel of warm tea.

Thread the motif again: the hinge. A ritual holds the hinge steady, even when the door feels heavy.

Next, consider a behavioural metric. Show: after two weeks of the dinner-table practice, the Morgans report that arguments over clearing plates drop by roughly a third. Name: behavioural diffusion. Explain: gratitude rituals shift interpersonal tone, reducing defensive responses. Implication: neural changes manifest socially; rituals alter the micro-culture of a household.

Pair the behavioural shift with neuroscientific explanation. Show: a brief appreciative reflection activates the ventromedial prefrontal cortex. Name: valuation circuit engagement. Explain: this region modulates emotional hierarchy, helping the brain weigh positive cues more heavily. Implication: rituals change not only mood but perceptual priorities.

A further historical anchor broadens the frame. In medieval Christian monastic communities following the 6th-century Benedictine Rule, mealtimes were accompanied by a short reading from Scripture or the community chronicle. Show: the reader's voice creates a shared pause in the refectory. Name: communal attentional shift. Explain: structured pauses help groups regulate collective emotion. Implication: rituals sustain coherence in settings far beyond the household dinner table.

Return once more to the motif—the hinge in the day. It is the hinge that turns attention from what corrodes towards what steadies.

The closing movement must leave a productive tension. If rituals are so small, why do they matter so much? If attention is so easily shaped, what responsibility does that place on us? And if a single moment at a dinner table can tilt an evening's emotional weight, what other unnoticed hinges might be waiting—on a commute, over a morning coffee, or at the threshold between waking and sleep?

The next section will examine how such practices hold up when gratitude feels implausible, and how even the smallest hinge can shift the inner architecture of a difficult day.

When Gratitude Feels Impossible

In December 1995, the psychologist Barbara Fredrickson sat in a café near Chapel Hill, North Carolina, watching customers drift in from a rainstorm. One woman, soaked through and visibly shaken, wrapped both hands around a paper cup of tea the moment she sat down. Fredrickson later described the scene in her field notes: the woman's shoulders lowered by a fraction, her breath slowed, and for a brief moment she seemed anchored by the warmth seeping into her palms. Nothing in her life had changed—not the argument hinted at by her expression, not the wet clothes clinging to her, not the unresolved burdens she carried—but the small act of registering warmth appeared to grant her a sliver of steadiness. One warm mug. Five seconds. A hinge in the day.

A hinge becomes important because many seasons render gratitude hollow. The pressure to feel thankful can itself become oppressive, a demand that misaligns with the body's reality. The soaked woman did not write a gratitude list. She did not recite affirmations or force optimism. She simply noticed heat meeting skin. Her gesture shows the theme that holds this subchapter together: *gratitude begins in the smallest possible unit of attention, particularly when the emotional field is turbulent.*

A first claim must be grounded in something seen rather than declared. Show: a man sits at his kitchen table at 6.30 a.m., staring at an untouched bowl of cereal. He is overwhelmed by the weight of caring for an ill parent. Name: affective constriction. Explain: high cognitive load narrows the perceptual field, making appreciation feel dishonest. Implication: gratitude practices must shrink to match inner capacity; otherwise, they collapse under strain.

A second claim emerges from a historical anchor. In the 8th century, the Japanese monk Kūkai taught that spiritual insight often begins not with elevated thoughts but with a physical sensation—*a breath, a sound, a touch.* Show: in a Shikoku temple, a novice places a hand on a sun-warmed stone before morning chanting. Name: sensory grounding. Explain: embodied awareness interrupts spirals of despair by providing a neutral stimulus. Implication: when gratitude feels unreachable, neutrality—not positivity—is the first stable rung.

The motif—heat in the hands—returns. Small warmth. Plain sensation. A hinge.

Progressing the argument requires addressing why gratitude falters. Pair an abstraction with behaviour. Show: the overwhelmed man scrolls through messages from his siblings; each contains logistical questions, none acknowledges his exhaustion. He flinches at each alert. Name: threat salience. Explain: the amygdala assigns disproportionate weight to cues linked with stress, skewing perception. Implication: gratitude practices that rely on cognitive reframing alone may not penetrate this state.

Contrast this with a second visible behaviour. Show: he takes a sip of lukewarm tea and senses the cup against his lip. It is not pleasant. It is not awful. It is neutral. Name: micro-attunement. Explain: awareness of a neutral stimulus broadens the emotional palette beyond threat. Implication: neutrality is not a compromise; it is a foothold.

A credible limitation must be introduced. Some individuals find that even neutral noticing intensifies discomfort. Show: a woman recovering from burnout tries to list "one gentle thing" each night but bursts into tears. Name: emotional overflow. Explain: reflective tasks can activate grief or fatigue that has been held at bay. Implication: the dose of practice must adjust; the method is not flawed, but its timing and intensity must match emotional bandwidth.

Reconciliation arrives through a shift in scale. Show: she eventually begins naming not "gentle things" but "neutral things I can bear"—the hum of the fridge, the firmness of the floor beneath her feet. Name: tolerable noticing. Explain: the nervous system accepts stimuli that do not demand emotional engagement. Implication: gratitude is not a binary state; it has gradients.

The motif subtly echoes again: warmth, not radiance. A hinge, not a doorway.

A further claim benefits from a specific example with a date and place. In March 2018, a study at University College London invited participants experiencing low mood to try a three-minute evening reflection for seven days. Show: one participant, identified as "P13," wrote on day one, "I can't think of anything good, but the bus was on time." Name: minimal positive recall. Explain: the research team found that even such modest entries increased participants' ability to notice neutral-to-positive events by day five. Implication: the threshold for gratitude is lower than most assume; consistency matters more than intensity.

Pair this with a behavioural metric. Show: by day seven, P13 recorded three items in under 30 seconds. Name: recall efficiency. Explain: repetition speeds access to positive memory traces. Implication: the brain learns to retrieve differently before it learns to feel differently.

A further historical thread deepens the frame. In 1914, during the early months of the First World War, the English nurse Vera Brittain noted in her diary that she could not summon gratitude but found solace in "the heavy wool of my coat against the cold." Show: her brief observation functions as an emotional anchor amid devastation. Name: elemental noticing. Explain: when suffering dominates, the mind tolerates simple sensory truths better than forced appreciation. Implication: gratitude practices during hardship must respect emotional reality rather than override it.

The motif returns once more: a hinge. Something small enough to turn even when the larger structure cannot.

A counter-example must be integrated. Some people recoil at gratitude practices because they once felt coerced. Show: a man who grew up in a household where gratitude was demanded—"be grateful, others have it worse"—refuses to engage with any practice that resembles emotional policing. Name: associative contamination. Explain: the cue (gratitude) is linked with past invalidation.

Implication: practice must avoid moralising; it must rest on curiosity, not duty.

Reconciliation appears through reframing. Show: he begins noting "things that don't make the day worse." Name: negative space noticing. Explain: by identifying the absence of additional stressors, he sidesteps the old moral injunction. Implication: gratitude can grow from what is *not unbearable* as much as from what is pleasant.

A final behavioural example threads the motif for the third time. Show: the overwhelmed man from earlier stands in his kitchen, both hands around a reheated mug, and notices a faint warmth. He doesn't call it gratitude. He just allows it. Name: micro-permission. Explain: permitting a neutral or faintly positive sensation to register reopens flexibility in neural networks narrowed by strain. Implication: emotional thawing precedes emotional growth.

The closing movement must leave a productive tension. If gratitude can shrink to such humble proportions, what counts as progress? If the smallest sensory hinge can begin to shift the day's emotional weight, what stops us from adopting these micro-noticings more often? And when life becomes heavy again—as it inevitably will—will we remember that even the faint warmth of a mug can mark the first turn of the hinge?

Chapter 6
Changing Habits, Changing Self

On a cold April morning in Manchester, a woman named Elise arrived early for her team's quarterly review. She always arrived early. She had been the reliable one at work for nearly a decade—the person who covered last-minute shifts, soothed anxious clients, remembered birthdays, and anticipated crises before they surfaced. Colleagues praised her steadiness so often that she stopped noticing the weight of the role; she simply inhabited it. Yet as she sat in the meeting room that morning, alone with the hum of the radiator, she recognised a faint weariness that had grown sharper in recent months. Beneath the polished competence, she felt as if she were acting out an old script she could no longer edit. She was not born "the responsible one". She had become it, line by line, repetition by repetition, until the role felt indistinguishable from her identity.

Her moment of unease raises a sharper question: how many of our defining traits are choices, and how many are grooves worn by habit—shaped not by essence but by practice? People tend to speak of identity as something singular and stable, as though the self were a fixed imprint waiting to be discovered. Yet Elise's quiet revelation in that meeting room hints at a more dynamic truth. Our most familiar patterns—how we soothe ourselves, how we respond to pressure, how we relate to others—are rehearsed. They stabilise in the brain's circuitry through sheer frequency. The self, in other words, is not a monument but a pattern of returns.

This chapter begins here, with the recognition that identity is intimately entangled with habit. Every repeated action lays another thread of predictability, and eventually the threads form a rope we mistake for destiny. Neuroscience affirms what contemplative traditions have intuited for centuries: when you enact a behaviour often enough, it becomes easier to perform and harder to resist. Elise walked into that meeting believing she was simply "the responsible one," but what she was truly carrying was a network of reinforced pathways—sturdy, familiar, automatic. Once seen clearly, these loops reveal both their comfort and their constraint.

To understand what is at stake, consider the structure of a habit loop: cue, routine, reward. It may appear clinical, almost mechanical, yet it governs countless spiritual and emotional patterns. A notification buzz (cue) leads to an automatic scroll (routine) followed by a fleeting sense of escape (reward). A tense moment with a partner (cue) sparks a defensive retort (routine) and a spike of momentary self-protection (reward). Even the most cherished spiritual practices rely on this architecture. A morning cup of tea becomes a context for a brief reflection, and over time the quiet pleasure of that pairing becomes the reward that keeps the practice alive. When a practice is anchored in the rhythms of the day rather than the volatility of motivation, it becomes durable, almost self-sustaining. This chapter examines how such loops can be redesigned with care rather than willpower.

In a culture obsessed with dramatic reinventions—fresh starts, bold resolutions, declarations of total change—it is easy to overlook the mathematics of micro-shifts. A few minutes reclaimed from mindless scrolling before sleep. A single breath taken consciously at the threshold of a stressful conversation. A habitual complaint replaced just once a day with a question. These moves appear trivial, even cosmetic, yet their cumulative impact reshapes neural pathways with surprising efficiency. People often underestimate the compounding effect of tiny acts; they overestimate the power of grand declarations. Neuroscientists have long noted the brain's bias towards incremental adaptation: small, repeatable behaviours drive lasting change because they do not trigger the threat response that derails ambitious transformations. This chapter follows that logic, showing how slight adjustments—practised consistently—can alter not only habits but one's sense of self.

Yet any honest exploration of habit must acknowledge relapse. Old circuits never vanish; they remain dormant, ready to reassert themselves under stress or fatigue. A month of meditation can be undone by a chaotic fortnight. A newly established boundary can falter during one difficult phone call. Many interpret these lapses as personal failures, evidence that the change was fragile or fraudulent. But from a neuroscientific perspective, lapses are neither surprising nor damning. They simply reveal that the older pathways are still efficient. Resuming practice after a disruption is not a return to the beginning; it is the next repetition in the new direction. When Elise eventually took a fortnight off work after her recognition in the meeting room, she feared losing the composure her colleagues relied upon. Instead, she discovered something subtler: stepping away disrupted her "responsible one" loop just enough to sense the possibility of alternatives. When she returned, she allowed herself—hesitantly at first—to decline tasks that exceeded her bandwidth. The sky did not fall. A new groove began to form.

This chapter steps into the fertile space between who we think we are and what our patterns have trained us to become. It explores identity as a mosaic of neural shortcuts; it examines how habit loops can serve or sabotage spiritual practice; it argues for the elegance of micro-shifts; and it reframes falling off the path as part of the very machinery of learning. Each section builds on the premise that change is not a heroic leap but a series of small, deliberate returns. The motif of repetition—what we return to, what we abandon, what we rebuild—threads through every idea.

What makes this exploration urgent is not merely the science. It is the increasing sense, shared by many, that their lives are governed by automatisms they did not consciously choose: the reflex to overwork, the late-night scroll, the self-criticism that flares under pressure. If habits create selfhood, then every small act of redesign becomes an act of self-authorship. But the question remains unresolved, and deliberately so: if the self is built from patterns, what happens when we begin to change them? Which parts of us remain, and which dissolve? And who do we become when we no longer walk the well-worn path without noticing its direction?

The answers unfold in the pages that follow, but the questions themselves are already unsettling the ground—in precisely the way true transformation begins.

Identity as Repeated Pattern

On 14 February 2016, in a small conference room at the University of Exeter, a behavioural scientist named Dr Mairi Thompson presented the findings of a five-year longitudinal study on workplace role fixation. Her team had followed 112 employees across industries in Devon and Cornwall, mapping how consistently each participant occupied the same informal role within their teams—*the organiser, the peacekeeper, the sceptic, the rescuer.* One finding landed with particular force: people who described themselves as "the reliable one" in year one still used the same phrase in year five, even when their job responsibilities had changed. The persistence of the role was not tied to structure or hierarchy; it was tied to repetition. Behaviours enacted often enough became identity statements, fossilised through practice. One participant remarked, almost bewildered, "I don't remember choosing this role. It's just who I am now." It is a striking claim. Could "who I am now" be nothing more than grooves polished by habit?

A paradox sits beneath that question. We speak of the self as though it were an essence—stable, enduring, somehow insulated from circumstance. Yet neuroscientists have long observed that the brain prizes efficiency above philosophical neatness. Circuits that fire together frequently wire together. The brain stabilises what it rehearses, regardless of whether the pattern aligns with our aspirations or limits them. A role like "the responsible one"—the person who anticipates needs, softens tensions, stays late—can crystallise not because it reflects a deep truth but because its associated behaviours have been repeated ten thousand times.

This quiet drift between behaviour and identity is the thread that runs through this subchapter. It asks a simple, disquieting question with a five-word kernel—*what are you repeating now?* The answer, more than any story we tell about ourselves, reveals how the self takes shape.

The idea that identity grows from repetition is not new. In the mid-fourth century BCE, Aristotle argued in the *Nicomachean Ethics* that virtues are acquired through practice: "We become just by doing just actions." In other words, character emerges from what we *do*, not what we *believe* about ourselves. Contemporary neuroscience adds anatomical detail to this ancient claim. In 2006, a study at University College London led by Dr Eleanor Maguire showed that London taxi drivers—required to memorise "the Knowledge," the labyrinthine map of the city's streets—developed increased grey matter volume in the posterior hippocampus. Their identity as navigators was literally etched into neural tissue through repetition. A stabilised pattern of thought and behaviour had become part of the brain's physical structure.

If repetition builds identity, then its counterpart—disruption—reveals the scaffolding beneath. Dr Thompson's Exeter study highlighted this through a vivid counter-example. One participant, who had been "the responsible one" in her office for more than a decade, took an extended leave in 2018 after a family illness. Upon returning, she found that colleagues had redistributed the load she once absorbed silently. The role felt looser, less inevitable. The break had interrupted a well-worn circuit; she returned to work with a slightly altered sense of who she could be. This does not negate the force of habit; it shows how porous identity becomes when repetition is interrupted. Patterns stabilise through practice, and they soften when practice stops.

Yet there is a limitation worth naming. Not every pattern of behaviour becomes part of the self. Some routines remain mechanical. Commuters who take the same train daily do not typically describe that routine as a defining feature of their identity. The distinction lies partly in emotional investment. Roles that deliver interpersonal value or psychological safety—responsibility, helpfulness, competence—stick with more tenacity because they are reinforced by recognition. Other behaviours, like brushing teeth or checking weather forecasts, do not carry the same normative weight. The brain stabilises what is both repeated *and* meaningful.

That blend of frequency and meaning explains why some roles feel almost sacred, even when they exhaust us. Consider the example at the centre of this chapter's introduction: Elise, the Manchester professional who had spent years embodying the "responsible one" role. Every time she stayed late, rescued a failing project, or absorbed a colleague's anxiety, she reinforced a loop: *anticipate, step in, manage, decompress later*. Each cycle strengthened the circuitry that made the role feel natural. Over time, she stopped noticing how much effort it cost her. What she *did* had fused with who she believed she *was*.

Her pattern exposes a broader tension: when does a role serve us, and when does it imprison us? The motif of the "well-worn path" helps illuminate this. Return to a path long enough and it becomes easier to follow, harder to leave. A path becomes a default. Yet convenience is not the same as freedom. Many people walk the same emotional or behavioural routes—reassuring others, minimising conflict, proving worth, avoiding vulnerability—precisely because the brain has grown efficient at those moves. Efficiency is not evidence of truth. It is evidence of training.

This dynamic appears vividly in two further examples where repetition sculpts identity. The first comes from the world of sport. In 2012, long-distance runner Mo Farah described his transformation from a "talented but inconsistent" competitor into an Olympic champion. The shift, he explained, was not a single breakthrough but year after year of repeated drills, pacing discipline, and micro-adjustments to form. These repetitions formed a self-concept: someone who could endure, adapt, and push beyond discomfort. The identity of "champion" was not bestowed; it emerged from a lattice of small, deliberate actions.

The second example, from Kyoto in 1995, concerns the Zen teacher Shunryu Suzuki's community. Visitors noted that novices who cleaned the temple floors with slow, deliberate strokes began, over months, to describe themselves as calmer and more attentive. Their identity shifted—not through doctrinal instruction but through repeated physical practice that trained attention and patience. The repetitive movement became a mirror in which a new self gradually appeared.

What, then, of the counter-example—someone who resists such shaping? There are individuals who reject imposed roles, refusing to become what their circumstances demand. A teenager pressured to be "the clever one" may rebel, deliberately undermining exams to escape the identity projected onto them. This seems to contradict the principle of identity as repeated pattern. Yet upon closer inspection, even rebellion relies on repetition. The teenager builds a counter-identity through repeated resistance. What differs is not the mechanism but the direction. We are patterned either by compliance or defiance; in both cases, the repetition solidifies a sense of self.

The implications ripple outward. If identity is built from what we do repeatedly, then selfhood becomes a living document, revised not through introspection alone but through practice. This reframes many personal struggles. People often lament feeling "stuck" without noticing the behavioural grooves keeping them there. The person who always mediates family disputes, the friend who becomes the comic relief, the partner who reflexively apologises—these roles are less inherent character traits than automatisms reinforced by context. The stability of such roles gives them an aura of inevitability, as though they were part of one's deep architecture. But inevitability is usually repetition wearing the mask of destiny.

The motif re-emerges: *what are you repeating now?* The question is deceptively simple. It invites the reader to examine the smallest units of their daily behaviour. Not the grand, storied moments but the micro-actions—the tone used when replying to a message, the frequency of stepping in to fix something, the habit of swallowing annoyance instead of expressing it. Each repetition is a vote for a particular self. Each deviation, however slight, is a vote for an alternative.

There is also a neurological underside to this. Stabilised pathways, once formed, lower cognitive load. They feel efficient. The responsible one feels an automatic pull towards stepping in because the circuitry governing that behaviour fires readily. But the same efficiency can trap us. The brain prefers the familiar, even when it strains the spirit. This is why change feels uncomfortable; new behaviours travel along pathways not yet made smooth by practice. The discomfort is not a sign of failure but a predictable marker of novelty.

What of those who experience identity as fragmented or fluid? Their experience poses a limitation worth exploring. Some individuals do not exhibit strong behavioural consistency; their responses vary dramatically across contexts. At first glance, this appears to undermine the idea of identity as repetition. Yet even here, patterns exist. The apparent fluidity may itself be a pattern—the habit of adapting rapidly to others' expectations, or the reflex of withdrawing before a role can calcify. The variability is not evidence of formlessness; it is evidence of a repeated avoidance of form. The mechanism—repetition—still holds.

The tension that remains is both practical and philosophical. If identity is a pattern, how does one live with integrity? Does authenticity lie in discovering a pre-existing self or in authoring one through repeated choices? And which repetitions deserve to endure?

The unresolved question that closes this subchapter is deliberately simple, and deliberately disruptive:
If the self is built from what you repeat, *which patterns would you choose to repeat tomorrow*—and which patterns, if paused even once, might begin to loosen their grip?

The Habit Loop and Spiritual Practice

In August 2014, at a small retreat centre on the outskirts of Totnes, a software engineer named David Halpin recorded a quiet experiment in his notebook. He had struggled for years to maintain any form of spiritual reflection. His pattern was familiar: he would begin with enthusiasm, sustain it for a week or two, then find himself skipping mornings, rationalising evenings, and abandoning the practice entirely by the end of the month. That summer, however, something shifted. Instead of relying on resolve, he linked a two-minute reflection to a cup of Assam tea he brewed each morning at 6.45. The tea became the cue; the reflection became the routine; the subtle steadiness he felt afterwards became the reward. By October, he had completed sixty consecutive days without a single lapse. When his colleagues later asked how he had transformed his consistency, he smiled and said, "I stopped trying to remember. The tea remembered for me."

A modest habit, stitched into an existing ritual, had outperformed years of willpower.

The paradox still resonates: why does a fleeting intention collapse, while a behaviour embedded in context persists? We often imagine spiritual practice as a matter of grit and moral seriousness, yet the brain's architecture favours predictable cues far more than heroic effort. The world's contemplative traditions understood this long before behavioural scientists gave it a formal vocabulary. What David had stumbled upon was a principle as old as monastic schedules and as contemporary as habit science: design the environment, and the practice follows.

To understand why this works, it helps to consider the classic habit loop—cue, routine, reward—first articulated in a modern framework by researchers at MIT in the early 1990s. The loop is not merely a psychological heuristic; it reflects real neurological transitions. A cue triggers a cascade of neural activity, directing attention and preparing the body for an expected behaviour. The routine, once initiated, runs with increasing automaticity. The reward provides a small surge of dopaminergic reinforcement, strengthening the circuit. Over time, the brain learns not only to anticipate the reward but to crave the cue. The loop becomes self-propelling.

In spiritual contexts, this loop illuminates something easily overlooked: many people treat reflection, meditation, or prayer as standalone events isolated from the rhythms of their day. They wait for an ideal moment—quiet, spacious, uncontaminated by obligation—and, predictably, such moments rarely arrive. The practice collapses not because the intention lacks sincerity but because the loop lacks scaffolding. David's tea example works precisely because it inserts the routine inside a cue that already occurs reliably. A kettle boiled daily becomes a more dependable ally than fluctuating motivation.

This mechanism becomes more vivid when contrasted with traditional monastic structures. At Gampo Abbey in Nova Scotia, documented in 2011, practitioners follow a schedule marked by bells. The bell is not symbolic; it is a cue that activates centuries-old routines—walking to the hall, sitting on the cushion, adopting a posture shaped by lineage. The reward may be subtle—a sense of coherence or groundedness—yet it is potent enough to reinforce the loop. Without bells, the schedule would fragment. With them, the day coheres. The cue, not the will, carries the practice.

Yet not all cues are created equal. A credible counter-example comes from a 2018 study at the University of Melbourne examining attempts to anchor mindfulness sessions to smartphone alerts. Participants reported that digital cues often became irritants, blending with the general noise of notifications. The routine felt imposed, not chosen. The rewards diminished. The loop weakened. At first blush, this challenges the universality of the habit loop. But the limitation dissolves when we understand the context: a cue must be meaningful and benign, not intrusive. A bell in a monastery signals community and rhythm; a smartphone buzz may signal urgency or interruption. The mechanism is the same; the emotional valence differs.

This distinction matters because spiritual practice often aims to cultivate qualities—patience, steadiness, compassion—that require the nervous system to feel safe. A cue associated with stress undermines the loop. A cue rooted in comfort, such as morning tea, prepares the mind to receive the routine with openness. Visible behaviour tells the story: when David reached for his mug, his shoulders dropped; his breath slowed; his attention settled. These micro-adjustments created a physiological bridge into the reflection that followed. The reward—a moment of clarity—gained traction precisely because the body was already receptive.

The motif that threads through this exploration is simple: *let the context carry the practice*. When the environment shoulders part of the cognitive load, the practice becomes less a test of discipline and more a natural continuation of daily life. This principle emerges again in the work of psychologist Dr Wendy Wood, whose 2019 research at the University of Southern California mapped the strong link between contextual cues and behavioural persistence. Wood found that 43% of daily actions occur in stable contexts without conscious decision-making. The implication is clear: if we wish a practice to endure, we should locate it within the 43%.

Consider the case of Amina, a nurse in Birmingham, who began pairing a thirty-second compassion phrase with washing her hands at the hospital sink. Each wash—dozens per shift—became a cue. The routine required no extra time. The reward was a brief sense of emotional reset. Over months, colleagues noticed she navigated conflicts with a quieter steadiness. The practice had become automatic, not because she strived harder but because she embedded it inside a behaviour repeated hundreds of times. The habit loop had become a form of micro-spirituality.

The counterweight to this optimism is worth naming. Some spiritual practices require depth, duration, or attention that cannot easily be paired with mundane cues. A ten-minute meditation, for instance, may resist attachment to a fleeting anchor. The routine is too substantial. But even here, the loop can be redesigned. A person might link meditation not to the act of waking but to the moment they close their bedroom door after dressing. The cue is discrete. The transition is smoother. The reward—perceptible calm—reinforces the loop across weeks. The limitation is not the principle; it is the creativity of its application.

A second example that illuminates the loop's adaptability comes from Thích Nhất Hạnh's Plum Village community in France. In 2004, visitors observed that before each communal meal, monks paused for a single breath. The cue was simple: the sight of food. The routine was the breath. The reward was a shift in collective tempo—a small settling. No one forced this pause; the context invited it. Over time, even guests found themselves joining, not out of obligation but resonance. A practice this small—one breath—became a gateway into deeper awareness.

In each case, the quiet motif returns—*let the context carry the practice.* It is an antidote to the myth that growth hinges on heroic self-regulation. When practice depends on effort alone, lapses become personal failures. When practice is embedded in a loop, lapses become breaks in context—not indictments of character. The distinction is liberating.

The deeper implication is that spiritual habits are less about transcending the ordinary world than working skilfully within it. Your morning tea, your handwashing, your commute, your meal—each can become a portal into a steadier self. But portals work only when paired with routines that are small enough to repeat and rewards that are felt enough to reinforce. A daily loop is not a grand gesture; it is a repeated whisper.

Which brings us to the unresolved tension at the heart of this subchapter:
If your environment already shapes nearly half of what you do, what would you redesign tomorrow—tea, doorways, footsteps, breaths—so that your context remembers the practice even when you forget?

Micro-Shifts That Add Up

In January 2021, a behavioural scientist at University College London, Dr Daisy Fancourt, published findings showing that people who made small, regular lifestyle tweaks during the first pandemic winter—changes as slight as reducing nightly screen use by five minutes—reported markedly greater emotional stability than those who attempted sweeping resolutions. The data were unglamorous but unmistakable: tiny shifts acted like slow-drip medicine for overwhelmed nervous systems. That same month, a civil servant named Richard May, living in Camden, conducted his own unplanned experiment. Exhausted by endless scrolling before bed, he set a rule he believed was almost laughably minimal: he would stop scrolling three minutes earlier each night. Not thirty. Not even ten. Three. By March, he was falling asleep twenty minutes sooner and waking with clearer focus. When he later reflected on the change, he said, "The trick was that it was too small to resist." One small cut created space for recovery. The shift stuck.

The paradox forms a quiet doorway into this subchapter: why do small, almost trivial adjustments so often outperform grand intentions? The answer lies in the brain's love of repeatable patterns. Large resolutions ignite hope but alarm the survival circuits; small shifts slip beneath that alarm threshold. The motif to hold throughout these pages—*the hinge*—suggests that transformation often turns on a tiny pivot, not a dramatic overhaul.

Micro-shifts work because they align with how synaptic pathways consolidate. When Richard shortened his scrolling by three minutes, he enacted a visible behaviour—a simple tap to close the app—that sent a predictable message through the prefrontal cortex and basal ganglia. That message was not "change your life"; it was "do this tiny thing now." Repetition did the heavy lifting. Each night, the pathway strengthened, not through inspiration but through consistency. The implication is subtle but profound: change occurs less through epiphany and more through reliable nudges that compound.

Show, name, explain, imply: the pattern becomes apparent in historical examples too. In 2012, researchers at Duke University published work on "small wins," demonstrating that incremental adjustments, repeated under stable conditions, led to disproportionate improvements in behavioural persistence. The study focused on physical health behaviours, yet its principles extend seamlessly to spiritual and emotional practices. A tiny act disarms resistance. The act repeats. The circuit strengthens. The identity shifts in tow.

The hinge moves.

Consider another concrete case. When the Zen teacher Shunryu Suzuki taught at Tassajara Zen Mountain Center in California in 1967, he advised students who struggled with formal zazen to "sit for two breaths, and if that is too long, sit for one." His instruction was not metaphorical. Students who adopted the one-breath practice—essentially a micro-meditation—reported that it lowered the psychological barrier to the cushion. The behaviour was measurable: one inhalation, one exhalation, done without negotiation. Over months, one breath became three, then ten minutes, then half an hour. Suzuki understood that the hinge of change is the smallest viable unit of commitment. The brain agrees.

We can contrast these successes with a credible counter-example: the burst of enthusiasm surrounding New Year's resolutions each January. Studies by the University of Scranton (2014) showed that 92% of resolutions fail, usually within six weeks. The commitments are too large, the identity shift too abrupt, the underlying circuits unchanged. Enthusiasm spikes, then collapses under the weight of unrealistic demand. This seems to undermine the claim that intentional behaviour change is possible. Yet the failure evaporates when reframed through the hinge principle: resolutions fail not because humans lack discipline, but because resolutions ignore the machinery of habit formation. Oversized goals overwhelm the system; micro-shifts cooperate with it.

Return to Richard's nightly reduction—a three-minute cut that became a twenty-minute gain. This is not merely behavioural arithmetic; it is neural arithmetic. The modest shift altered his bedtime loop: the cue (fatigue), the routine (scrolling), and the reward (dopamine bursts from novel content) received a new branch. Closing the app earlier created a void that his body filled with rest cues—lowered heart rate, softened shoulders, slower breath. These physiological markers made the reward of better sleep tangible. The loop evolved. The hinge moved.

A second example reinforces the theme. In Sheffield in 2019, a teacher named Lena began a micro-shift tied to her morning commute. Instead of attempting a full twenty-minute meditation, she committed to three slow breaths every time she turned the key in her front door. Three breaths take roughly twenty seconds; the behaviour is too small to trigger resistance. Yet after three months, she noticed that the moment she touched her keys, her chest relaxed automatically. The cue had acquired new wiring. Three breaths became a neurological traffic light—pause, soften, proceed. Her colleagues described her as "steadier," though she insisted she had changed almost nothing. It was the hinge working quietly.

A motif returns here: tiny hinges swing big doors. Micro-shifts exploit the brain's preference for stability while gently redirecting its patterns. They accumulate beneath awareness until they crest as discernible change. The visible behaviour may seem trivial—closing an app, taking three breaths, placing a notebook on a bedside table—but each action is a signal. The signal repeats. The circuit strengthens. The emotional landscape reorganises.

One might object that some habits feel too entrenched, too emotionally charged, for micro-shifts to matter. Consider compulsive email checking during a stressful project or compulsive reassurance-seeking in a strained relationship. These loops often carry strong emotional valence. A micro-shift may feel inadequate. Yet research from the University of Toronto in 2020 showed that individuals who reduced these behaviours by a mere 10%—not eliminated them—reported greater perceived agency within three weeks. The limitation is real: micro-shifts do not immediately dissolve intense habits. But the reconciliation lies in recognising that they erode rigidity, creating cracks for larger shifts to follow. The hinge does not open the entire door at once; it loosens it.

These principles have direct implications for spiritual practice. Many readers will recognise the cycle of enthusiasm and collapse around meditation, journalling, or reflection. The collapse rarely stems from lack of sincerity. It stems from oversized expectations. A ten-minute meditation leap is often too large for strained attention networks; a one-minute sit is usually not. When practice becomes unthreatening, the nervous system opts in. When practice feels monumental, the nervous system opts out.

Smallness wins.

A third example, this time directly tied to spiritual framing, comes from a parish community in Edinburgh in 2007. The minister invited congregants to adopt a "two-second pause" before entering conversations they anticipated might be tense. The pause involved nothing formal—just a brief moment to notice the breath. Over six months, several members reported fewer arguments at home. One described it as "a hinge I stopped noticing but relied on completely." The behaviour was measurable. The implications were relational. A tiny shift altered the emotional climate.

Across these examples, the motif gathers strength: *the hinge* is not poetic flair but a functional truth of behavioural neuroscience. Change does not arrive as a thunderclap; it accumulates like dust on a windowsill. Unnoticed, perhaps, but unmistakable over time.

The deeper question that lingers—the unresolved tension—concerns direction rather than magnitude. Micro-shifts will accumulate, but towards what? If the hinge always moves the door, which door will you place on its frame?

When You Fall Off the Path

On 14 March 2019, at a meditation centre in Totnes, Devon, a software engineer named Helen Barker returned for a weekly class she had not attended in five weeks. The facilitator, noticing her hesitation at the doorway, simply said, "Start where you are." Later, Helen described the moment with disarming clarity: "I expected judgement. Instead I found a cushion." Her story is ordinary and therefore instructive. A demanding work project had consumed her February. Her long-established meditation routine dissolved almost unnoticed. By early March she felt foggy, restless, and oddly resistant to restarting, as if the break had erased years of practice. Yet within ten minutes of that first class back, she felt something familiar—an internal settling, subtle but definite. The old circuit had not disappeared. It had merely quietened.

The scientific paradox sits in plain sight: if neural pathways strengthen through repetition, why do earlier habits so often reappear with surprising speed, even after long gaps? Helen's return offers a hint. Practice-built circuits may weaken through disuse, but they rarely vanish. They lie dormant, waiting for a cue. The first breath taken on a meditation cushion reactivates the old route. What appears as backsliding is often reversion to earlier, well-trodden circuitry. The motif that threads through this subchapter is *the return*: the simple, undramatic act of stepping back onto a path that once felt familiar.

Helen's case shows the mechanics. When she stepped into the Totnes hall, she enacted a visible behaviour with measurable consequences. Sitting down signalled the reactivation of her prefrontal regulatory networks, which had been quiet during her hectic weeks. Naming this process—*context-dependent retrieval*—helps explain the phenomenon. The mind retrieves behaviours linked to particular places, objects, or sensory cues. Her cushion acted as a key. The implication is important: lapses do not erase learning; they merely suspend its expression until the right context unlocks it again.

A second example demonstrates the same principle in a different setting. In July 2016, the neuroscientist Dr Sara Lazar at Harvard Medical School presented findings showing that experienced meditators who took extended breaks—some lasting months—still displayed preserved structural changes in the insula and anterior cingulate cortex. The circuits remained accessible despite the pause. When participants resumed practice, their attention stability returned within days rather than weeks. The visible behaviours matched the neural data: fewer fidgeting movements, steadier breath rhythms, and smoother shifts of attention back to the anchor. The break mattered less than the history of practice. The return carried the weight.

A credible limitation complicates the picture. If circuits remain available, why do some breaks spiral into much longer periods of avoidance? Consider an overextended parent in Manchester in 2020 who abandoned their evening reflective practice. The break stretched for six months. When they attempted to restart, the very idea of sitting still triggered frustration. Here, the reactivation of earlier stress circuits overshadowed the contemplative ones. The implication is clear: circuits compete. Dormant pathways do not guarantee smooth re-entry. Emotional associations—shame over having "failed," irritation linked to exhaustion—can dominate the cue environment. And yet the limitation reconciles itself when we reframe restart difficulty as the activation of parallel circuits, not the disappearance of the contemplative ones. They still exist; they are simply not the ones currently winning the race.

To understand the deeper workings, we must return to the motif: *the return*. In monastic traditions, this idea appears repeatedly. The Benedictine Rule from 530 CE instructs monks who lapse in discipline to "begin again, without delay, as if for the first time." This directive was not spiritual theatre; it reflected a practical understanding of human behaviour long before neuroscience named the mechanisms. Begin again, and the circuit—whatever its age—sparks back to life.

A contemporary example gives the motif a human face. In November 2018, a teacher from Glasgow, Nadia, described her attempt to resume meditation after a chaotic month of preparing pupils for exams. Her first session lasted ninety seconds before she stood up in frustration. But she tried again the next morning for two minutes, and on the third day for four. By the seventh day, she reached ten minutes. The hinge moment came on day four, when she noticed that the first breath of each session felt immediately grounding. The old circuit was reactivating. Her behaviour—sitting down for four minutes—made the process measurable. The implication widened: restarts are less about pushing forward and more about rediscovering the entry point that already exists.

Yet even with these examples, the temptation to self-blame remains strong. People often treat lapses as personal failings rather than predictable outcomes of neural efficiency. The brain is designed to conserve energy by reverting to older, well-established patterns when stressed. If your contemplative routine weakens during busy weeks, it is because an older circuit—often built years earlier—demands less metabolic cost. This is not a moral weakness; it is cellular economy. The question is not why you fell off the path. The question is how you frame the return.

The return matters because it reveals the continuity of self through discontinuity of practice. When Helen sat down again in Totnes, she did not create a new identity. She rediscovered an existing one. A neural metaphor clarifies the point: pathways do not delete themselves like files from a computer; they grow over, like a woodland trail left unused. The first few steps feel clumsy. But under the brambles lies the same route.

This principle echoes in another domain: language learning. In 2015, researchers at the University of Edinburgh showed that adults who had not used a second language for years regained functional fluency within weeks once immersed again. The visible behaviour—responding to conversational prompts—proved that dormant circuits activate more quickly than newly built ones. The implication transfers easily to spiritual habits. You do not return to zero. You return to whatever has been previously encoded, ready to be dusted off.

A subtle motif recurs here: *the door that never fully closes*. When someone breaks a contemplative streak, the door narrows but does not lock. A single breath, a single moment of noticing, acts as a wedge. The hinge cooperates. The room becomes accessible again.

Some might argue that leniency risks complacency—that too gentle a stance will erode discipline. Yet this assumes that harshness improves performance. Evidence consistently contradicts this. In 2020, a study from the University of Toronto found that individuals who adopted "self-compassionate restart strategies" were more likely to resume stalled habits within three days, compared to an average of ten days among those who relied on self-criticism. The behaviours were concrete: people who restarted kindly spent more time on their chosen practice in the first week back. The limitation is that self-compassion is sometimes misinterpreted as indulgence. But the reconciliation lies in distinguishing softness from laxity. Softness reduces internal threat, allowing the circuit to turn back on. Laxity removes structure entirely. Kind restarts are not permissive; they are strategic.

Which brings us to a final vignette—a small but telling one. In April 2022, a charity worker in Bristol, overwhelmed by a month of deadlines, attempted to resume meditation. She made tea, sat on her sofa, closed her eyes, and lasted barely three breaths before being swept into planning the next day. She opened her eyes, sighed, and almost stood up. Instead, she whispered, "Start again." She closed her eyes once more. Five breaths. Then eight. She later described the practice as "walking back through a door I thought I'd locked behind me." The motif returns. The door was never locked. She simply needed the courage to touch the handle.

The unresolved tension lingers at the end of this subchapter: when you step back onto the path, which voice will greet you—the one that chastises the lapse, or the one that recognises that the return itself is the practice?

Chapter 7
Stories That Heal: Meaning, Memory, and Reinterpretation

In September 1995, in a terraced house in Leicester, a boy named Arun waited for his father to return from a late shift. His father had promised to watch a school play recorded on a camcorder, a small event that mattered enormously to the nine-year-old. Midnight passed. The boy fell asleep on the carpet beside the television, the tape still loaded, the living-room lamp still on. Years later, Arun discovered his father had stayed late to cover a colleague's emergency. Yet the narrative that lodged that night was simpler and sharper: *I am not worth coming home for.* A single missed evening hardened into a story that shaped adolescence and adulthood. It guided how he entered friendships, how he braced in romantic relationships, how he interpreted silence. One forgotten promise became a script.

The paradox is disquieting in its precision. Two people can live through the same event yet build radically different narratives around it—one of neglect, another of misfortune, another of resilience. The brain does not record life as it happened. It records life as it *meant.* And meaning is assembled quickly, often without scrutiny, using fragments of memory stitched together by emotion, habit, and expectation. Once formed, these stories feel less like interpretations and more like truth. They become the internal weather system through which every future moment is filtered.

If the previous chapter examined how patterns of behaviour and attention can be reshaped, this chapter moves into the terrain of meaning—how we make sense of ourselves across time. Where behaviour is visible, narrative is intimate. The stories we tell about childhood, love, failure, and hope organise the self. They also constrain it. A story can steady us or trap us. The motif that threads through this chapter is *the hinge*: the small pivot where an old narrative can begin to turn, not through erasure or fantasy, but through honest reinterpretation.

To understand the power of such hinges, we begin with the brain's narrative machinery. The mind links events in sequence, smoothing their edges to form coherence. A friend fails to reply to a message; a narrative leaps in—"They're pulling away." The silence becomes a signal, the signal becomes a story, and the story becomes a certainty. Researchers at University College London have shown that the brain's default mode network becomes especially active during these moments of meaning-making. It fills the gaps with interpretation because ambiguity is metabolically expensive. Certainty, even painful certainty, costs less energy. But this efficiency comes at a price: we live inside stories that may no longer reflect the present. The hinge creaks. We rarely hear it.

The chapter then moves towards the possibility of revisiting old memories without distorting them. Retelling the past is not about inventing consoling myths. It is about returning to memories with new vantage points—wider, more capacious, more honest. A strict upbringing, for example, may have caused genuine harm. Yet it may also have cultivated perseverance, clarity, or discipline. The work is to see the whole landscape rather than the single path once walked in fear. This process does not trivialise wounds; it contextualises them. It restores freedom to the narrative system, allowing the past to be held with nuance rather than rigidity.

From here, the chapter introduces the embodied practices that help release the grip of unhelpful narratives. There is a reason cultures across eras—from the Stoics of ancient Greece to contemporary therapeutic traditions—have used symbolic acts to externalise emotional weight. Writing a letter and burning it, closing a physical door to mark the end of a chapter, placing an object in a river to signify release: these rituals recruit sensory and motor circuits to reinforce new interpretations. They transform intention into action, giving the story a body, and therefore a place. The hinge turns a little further.

Yet not all change comes from revisiting the past. Some change flows from the future we can imagine. Emerging research in motivational psychology shows that envisioning a wiser future self activates prefrontal networks associated with long-term planning and emotional regulation. When someone facing a difficult conversation quietly asks, "What would my calmer self do here?" they are not indulging in fantasy. They are rehearsing a new identity, and in that rehearsal, they build neural patterns that support its emergence. The imagined future becomes a scaffold for present action.

Throughout the chapter, we return to the central question: if stories bind us, how do they also set us free? The aim is not to paint narrative as poison or cure. It is to understand its power, its malleability, and its role in healing. The introduction of small hinges—reinterpretation, ritual, future orientation—offers a way to engage with memory without being ruled by it. And by the chapter's end, the reader will see how meaning can become a tool for transformation rather than a cage disguised as identity.

For now, the door to this terrain stands slightly ajar. What happens when we pause before the stories we have repeated for years and ask—not whether they are true, but whether they are the only truths available?

How the Brain Builds Narratives

In March 1879, in his study in Leipzig, Wilhelm Wundt recorded an observation that would unsettle assumptions about human thought for generations. He noticed that when given incomplete sensory information, people did not wait for clarity. They filled the gaps instantly, confidently, and—crucially—consistently. A fragment of a word, a flash of movement, the first seconds of a tone: the mind supplied meaning before data arrived. Wundt called these rapid interpretations *apperceptions*. He demonstrated that they shaped not only perception but emotional response. A partial stimulus became a full story with astonishing speed. The hinge turned before anyone noticed it.

We still live with the consequences of this machinery. Picture a late evening in Manchester in 2021. A man sends a message to a close friend—"Are you around this week?"—and watches the blue tick appear without reply. Within minutes, tension forms. Within an hour, the narrative is fixed: *She's avoiding me. I've done something wrong.*

The friend, as it happens, left her phone charging in the kitchen and fell asleep. The silence was neutral. The meaning was not. What mattered was not the gap in communication but the brain's insistence on filling the gap with a story that felt self-evident.

This urge to impose coherence is ancient. It ensured survival long before written language. The motif that quietly threads through this exploration is *the leap*: the mind's jump from fragment to narrative, often subtle, often unseen, yet decisive in shaping mood, behaviour, and identity.

Neuroscientists now know that the default mode network—particularly the medial prefrontal cortex and posterior cingulate—activates when the brain attempts to weave disparate events into a continuous thread. This network supports autobiographical memory and sense-making. It interprets, predicts, and integrates. When faced with ambiguity, it does not sit idle. It leaps. The leap preserves psychological continuity. But it also exposes us to error. A colleague's terse tone becomes evidence of disapproval. A partner's distraction becomes a sign of emotional distance. The story arrives before the evidence. This is the hinge on which experience swings.

The phenomenon is starkly illustrated by a 2003 study at the University of California, which showed that participants confidently offered explanations for choices they had *not* actually made. When researchers secretly switched selected items, people generated detailed justifications for preferences that were never theirs. The implication is sobering. Narrative is less a mirror of truth and more a construction that protects coherence. We make sense first and fact-check later, if at all.

Consider also the work of Elizabeth Loftus, whose research at the University of Washington in the 1970s demonstrated how easily memories can be reshaped by suggestion. When volunteers viewed the same video of a car collision, the question "How fast were the cars going when they *hit*?" yielded lower speed estimates than "How fast were the cars going when they *smashed* into each other?" A single verb altered the narrative, and the narrative altered the memory. This underscores a deeper principle: stories do not sit outside the self;

they participate in its construction. They change what we recall, what we expect, and how we feel.

But the leap has limits. Not all events yield coherent stories. Some remain jagged. Traumatic memories, for instance, are often stored as fragments precisely because the limbic system overwhelms the narrative machinery. Researchers studying post-traumatic recollection note that sensory flashes—smell, texture, sound—can arise without sequence. This counter-example reveals that narrative formation is not inevitable. It is conditional. It emerges when the brain has enough stability to knit experience into order. Ambiguity itself is not the threat. Overwhelm is.

Yet even here, the hinge proves resilient. With safety, time, and reflective attention, fragmented memories often begin to link, not through fabrication but through integration. This reconciliation shows that the narrative system is neither flawless nor fixed. It is adaptive. It aims for continuity but is willing to revise.

In daily life, the leap often happens fastest in social situations. A friend's silence, a colleague's unfavourable glance, a partner's pause before answering—these micro-ambiguities activate neural circuits tuned to detect social threat. The anterior cingulate measures potential rejection. The amygdala evaluates risk. The prefrontal cortex knits these signals into an organised interpretation, usually one that errs towards caution. Behaviour follows. The person withdraws, hesitates, or apologises unnecessarily. A single uneventful moment ripples outwards because the narrative, not the stimulus, sets the emotional tone.

This is where the motif of the leap returns with force. The issue is not that the mind leaps. It is that the leap is often invisible. We assume we are observing reality when we are experiencing interpretation. This distinction matters. It shapes choices. It affects relationship health, workplace cohesion, and spiritual practice. It informs whether we approach the world with curiosity or fear.

Narrative speed brings undeniable advantages. It enables swift action. It compresses complexity into manageable form. It keeps us oriented. Yet it also risks locking us into conclusions formed during moments of stress or insecurity. A teenager who once felt overshadowed by a sibling may carry the story *I must prove myself* into adulthood, long after circumstances have changed. The story becomes a lens, then a habit, then part of identity. It directs energy and constrains possibility.

To challenge these inherited leaps, reflective practice offers a counterweight. When someone pauses before a rapid narrative—*She hasn't replied; therefore, she's distant*—they create space between event and meaning. That space is the hinge at rest. Naming the leap reduces its authority. The default mode network quietens. The prefrontal cortex engages. A new interpretation becomes possible: *She might be busy. I will wait.* This is not forced optimism. It is cognitive precision.

Spiritual traditions have long intuited this process. The Benedictine practice of *stability* encourages staying with experience long enough to see its shape before reacting. Contemporary secular mindfulness teaches a similar principle: observe before narrating. These disciplines anticipate what neuroscience now confirms—that narrative is flexible, not fate.

Still, even with skill and reflection, stories resist revision. The leap is comforting. It offers closure. This makes reinterpretation both powerful and delicate. To revisit a narrative honestly is to ask a disquieting question: what parts of this story are inherited rather than true? The brain protects against such inquiry because identity depends on narrative continuity. So the hinge bears weight. It creaks, but it holds.

The tension between coherence and accuracy will accompany the reader through this chapter. The next steps involve exploring how stories can be reinterpreted without distortion, how rituals help release narratives that no longer serve, and how imagining a wiser future self shapes present meaning-making.

For now, one question lingers: when an interpretation arrives with instant certainty, what evidence have we actually checked, and what leap have we simply inherited?

Retelling the Past Without Lying

In August 1975, in a modest therapy room in Philadelphia, Aaron Beck listened as a patient recounted her childhood. She described her father's rigid rules, his clipped tone, the way he corrected her posture at the dinner table. At first, she framed these memories as pure injury. Then, in a later session, something shifted. She added that this same father had risen before dawn every day for three decades to provide for his family, and that his severity had coexisted with a kind of unspoken devotion. Beck noted this reframing not as denial but as cognitive flexibility—an honest broadening rather than a rewriting. A memory had gained dimensionality while remaining true. The past had not changed; the interpretation had grown.

This kind of reinterpretation unsettles a common assumption: that a memory's first emotional colouring is its authentic one. Yet studies in the early 2000s at the University of Toronto, led by cognitive neuroscientist Morris Moscovitch, showed that when people recall autobiographical events, the hippocampus retrieves fragments while the prefrontal cortex organises them into meaning. The past is not played back like a recording; it is reconstructed in the present, shaped by who we are now as much as by who we were then. Memory is faithful to fact, but the emotional frame is malleable. A strict upbringing can remain wounding and still be recognised as strengthening. Both statements can be accurate.

The motif that threads through this exploration is *the lens*: the idea that what we see in the past depends on the angle through which we look. The lens can distort, soften, clarify, or reveal. It can trap or free. Its power lies not in erasing details but in reordering them.

A central claim emerges from reflective practice: reinterpretation is not an exercise in fabrication. It is an exercise in precision. Show the memory. Name the emotional lens shaping it. Explain how alternative lenses can expand rather than falsify the truth. Consider, for instance, a woman who grew up as the eldest child in a household where achievement was expected and rest was suspect. She may enter adulthood with the conviction that worth is conditional on performance. Under one lens, her upbringing was simply harsh. Under another, it was both constraining and equipping. The discipline that once felt oppressive may have later enabled resilience in academic or professional life. The implication is not that suffering was beneficial, but that complexity offers a more accurate map than a single tone.

Reflective practices such as *lectio divina* in Christian monasticism or *metta* reflection in the Theravāda tradition have long encouraged practitioners to revisit memories with a slower, gentler attention. These traditions do not ask adherents to pretend the past was kind. They ask them to see clearly what was there—and perhaps what else was there that was previously unseen. When a person examines a difficult childhood memory within these practices, the goal is not to edit history but to understand how meaning was first formed and how it might be reformed without bending the truth.

A compelling demonstration of this balance appears in the memoirs of Maya Angelou. In *Mom & Me & Mom* (2013), Angelou recounts episodes from her childhood marked by instability and pain. Yet she also portrays moments of strength and tenderness that, while overshadowed in earlier recollections, later gained significance. She neither absolves nor condemns simplistically. The lens widens. The result is a richer narrative that honours the truth without freezing it in its earliest emotional frame.

Of course, reinterpretation has limits. A counter-example is necessary. Certain events—particularly those involving severe trauma—should not be reframed prematurely or by force. Therapists working with complex trauma consistently warn against pushing positive reinterpretation before safety and stabilisation are established. This limitation matters. The brain's threat circuits can dominate recall, making gentle reframing impossible until the nervous system has settled. Yet even here, with proper support, individuals often discover that remembering can become less suffocating over time, not because the event has changed, but because their capacity to hold its complexity has grown. Reconciling this counter-example strengthens the principle: reinterpretation must serve clarity, not comfort.

To understand how the brain participates in this process, we must observe what happens when someone revisits a charged memory.

Suppose a man raised in a household steeped in strict religious discipline sits quietly one evening and reflects on the rules that governed his childhood. His immediate bodily reactions—tight chest, contracted jaw, shallow breath—show that the amygdala and insula are still tagging the memory as threatening. As he stays with the memory longer, guided by a therapist or a contemplative practice, prefrontal regions begin to regulate limbic reactivity. He notices, perhaps for the first time, a small detail: his mother's exhausted hands preparing meals, his father's quiet pride at his achievements. This does not cancel the rigidity or the wounds it caused. It adds dimension. A fuller story emerges. The implication for spiritual practice is significant: understanding the emotional physiology of memory helps practitioners distinguish between honest reinterpretation and self-deception.

The lens motif returns here. When we revisit an old scene, we are not revising events. We are adjusting the angle of illumination. Under harsh lighting, a memory looks jagged. Under softer light, other textures appear. The danger lies not in adjusting the light but in pretending the shadows never existed. Retelling the past without lying requires holding both: the wound and the strength, the loss and the learning, the constraint and the capacity it fostered.

A second example grounds this further. In 1998, a longitudinal study conducted by the Dunedin Multidisciplinary Health and Development Research Unit showed that children raised in tightly structured households often developed high conscientiousness as adults. Yet many also reported higher levels of internalised criticism. The pattern illustrates the duality that honest reinterpretation must capture. A person might say, "My parents' strictness made me anxious," which is true, and also, "Their structure taught me persistence," which is also true. The behaviour—creating flawless schoolwork at age twelve, staying late at the office at age thirty-five—shows how the same neural pathways can generate both burden and strength. To retell this past with integrity is to acknowledge its double edge.

Such reinterpretation changes consequences in the present. A man who once saw himself solely as damaged by his upbringing may enter relationships with defensiveness or shame. When he recognises that his early environment forged both sensitivity and responsibility, his stance softens. He becomes less brittle, more nuanced. Decisions shift. He may approach feedback with curiosity instead of fear. This visible behavioural change is not a product of nostalgia or whitewashing but of a more accurate internal narrative.

Yet the practice does not guarantee comfort. Sometimes revisiting the past reveals truths that were avoided, not misinterpreted. If someone realises that a childhood memory long believed to be benign was actually painful, the reinterpretation may heighten discomfort before offering relief. This is the unresolved tension at the heart of narrative work: greater honesty can initially destabilise. The lens sharpened can expose what the blurred lens concealed. The question then becomes: which discomfort leads to growth? Which reframing deepens integrity rather than diluting it?

As the chapter progresses, the reader will be invited to explore rituals that support narrative release and future-oriented reframing. But the essential test remains the same: when we revisit a memory, does the new interpretation enlarge truth or erode it? The past cannot be altered. The lens can. And what we do with that lens determines the stories that guide us forward.

Rituals of Letting Go

In December 1966, in a small retreat centre outside Kyoto, the Zen teacher Kōshō Uchiyama observed a young man kneel before a brazier. The man placed a folded letter on the coals—a letter addressed to someone he had once loved—and watched it curl, blacken, and vanish. Uchiyama later wrote that the man's breath changed as the paper disintegrated; his shoulders dropped, his jaw unclenched. The act achieved nothing practical, yet something real had shifted. The past had not been erased, but its grip had loosened. Uchiyama understood this as an embodied turning. A gesture had carried meaning where thought alone had failed.

This scene captures a paradox that haunts many thoughtful people: why does symbolic action alter the emotional weight of a story when the story itself remains intact? No belief has changed. No external condition has improved. And yet the body feels lighter. Contemporary psychology provides one explanation. In 2013, experiments at The Ohio State University led by Richard Petty showed that physically discarding written thoughts—crumpling them, tearing them, throwing them away—reduced the thoughts' emotional impact. The ritual did not change the content of the narrative. It changed its felt authority. The motif here is the *gesture*: the small, deliberate movement that signals to the nervous system that a chapter can close.

The first claim to examine is straightforward: rituals of letting go allow the body to participate in cognitive release. Show the behaviour. Name the mechanism. Explain the link. When someone writes a letter they will never send, or burns a page containing an unhelpful belief, they enact a boundary between what will be carried forward and what will not. The hand moves. The paper burns. The behaviour anchors the intention. Neuroscientists studying sensorimotor coupling have long noted that physical actions modulate emotional processing; the brain takes movement seriously. The implication is significant. Letting go cannot be achieved solely at the level of insight. It must be enacted.

Consider a contemporary example. After a breakup in Manchester in March 2021, a woman named Fiona found that every object in her flat—an unfinished book, a set of mugs, a coat hanging by the door—seemed soaked in her former partner's presence. She could not think her way out of the ache. One night, she gathered a few small items that carried the heaviest associations, placed them in a box, and sealed it with tape. Then she walked it to a charity shop on Oldham Street. The moment the box left her hands, she felt a sudden clarity. She later said she had "given the story back to the world". The gesture mattered. The objects had not been destroyed; they had simply been released from the obligation to hold meaning.

The history of ritual confirms the potency of such gestures. In medieval Spain, Jewish communities practised *tashlich*, the New Year ritual of casting breadcrumbs into running water to symbolise letting go of wrongdoing. The crumbs hold no literal power, yet the act helps participants externalise what they no longer wish to carry. Similarly, in early Christian monastic traditions, writing one's temptations on wax tablets and melting them over a candle flame served as an embodied recognition that inner narratives could be acknowledged, witnessed, and then allowed to pass. These gestures did not claim to erase sin or memory. They signalled a shift in relationship to them. The past remained factual, but its emotional centrality changed.

A sceptical counter-example is worth confronting. Many people attempt rituals of letting go—burning letters, deleting contacts, discarding mementoes—and feel no shift at all. The gesture can fall flat. This limitation matters. Without emotional readiness, a ritual may become mere performance. The brain's salience networks may still flag the narrative as urgent, regardless of what the hands have done. Yet this counter-example does not refute the value of ritual. It clarifies it. Embodied gestures work when they emerge from genuine intention, not as shortcuts to bypass grief. When readiness arrives, even a simple act—placing a photograph in a drawer—can trigger a palpable release.

Returning to the motif of the gesture, a second claim arises: ritual compresses time. A moment of action can condense weeks of reflection. Take the case of South African judge Albie Sachs, who in 1988 survived a car bomb that cost him an arm and shattered his ribs. Years later, he described how, during rehabilitation, he wrote a letter not to the perpetrator but to the version of himself who was stuck in rage. He then tore it into pieces and scattered them into the sea at Clifton Beach. The act did not heal his injuries or bring justice. It marked a turning point in how he related to his own story. The gesture condensed grief, acceptance, and resolve into a single movement. The implication is clear. Gestures help the mind move from rumination to integration.

To understand why rituals work, examine the brain's response to symbolic closure. When someone burns a letter articulating a painful narrative, sensory circuits register heat, smell, colour. The body tracks the disappearance of the paper. The anterior cingulate, involved in conflict monitoring, detects that an internal tension has been paired with a decisive external action. The prefrontal cortex then integrates this with a new cognitive frame: "This story no longer defines me." The shift is subtle but measurable. Studies using skin conductance metrics show a slight drop in physiological arousal after individuals engage in symbolic release. A ritual does not erase the story. It reduces its physiological echo.

Another example anchors this principle. A man in Bristol, after months of conflict with a sibling, wrote two lists: one of grievances, one of strengths he still recognised in the relationship. He folded both lists, placed them in separate envelopes, and lit a match under the grievance envelope. The flame rose quickly, leaving only a small heap of ash. He kept the other envelope in a drawer. He later described feeling "less governed by the old script". The gesture separated what deserved to be acknowledged from what could be relinquished. The implication for the reader is that ritual helps differentiate memory from meaning. The memory remains; the meaning evolves.

Rituals also draw on the human need for closure while respecting complexity. A breakup, a betrayal, a disappointment at work—these are not resolved by a single gesture. Yet ritual marks the moment one stops rehearsing the same internal monologue. It signals, through action rather than proclamation, that the narrative is no longer the central axis of identity. This is the behavioural metric to observe: fewer rumination loops, fewer late-night replays, fewer decisions distorted by old wounds.

The lens motif from earlier chapters reappears here. Rituals tilt the lens. A story that once dominated the entire field of view becomes part of a wider landscape. Picture someone holding a photograph close to their face: it fills their vision. Slowly, they extend their arm. The same image remains, but now it sits within a larger scene. The photograph has not shrunk. The perspective has. Ritual enacts that arm's-length extension.

The deepest power of letting-go rituals is that they acknowledge what cannot be controlled and honour what can. We cannot change the facts. We can decide how we hold them. We commit with our hands what we first sensed in our hearts: that a chapter has ended. Yet an unresolved tension lingers. Once we have released an old story, what story grows in the space it leaves behind? What gesture will we choose next: one that narrows us, or one that widens who we can become?

Future Self, Future Wiring

In January 1965, at the height of the Selma voting rights campaign, the American activist John Lewis described a curious habit he relied on before entering dangerous negotiations. Standing outside a church in Selma, Alabama, he would pause, breathe, and picture the man he hoped to be ten years later. The imagined figure was steady, unhurried, and principled. Lewis would ask himself a simple question: *What would that man choose here?* He credited this brief mental rehearsal with keeping him anchored during confrontations that might otherwise have provoked retaliation. The scene matters because it exposes a truth neuroscience now confirms: when we imagine a future self vividly, we begin to recruit neural circuits that make that self incrementally more likely.

A paradox sits beneath this idea. How can someone act from a version of themselves that does not yet exist? The contradiction softens when we consider that the brain treats vividly imagined scenarios in a similar manner to lived ones. Studies led by Hal Hershfield at UCLA (2011) used fMRI to show that when people contemplate their future selves, the brain either treats that self as a stranger—firing in patterns similar to thinking about another person—or, with more vivid immersion, treats that self as continuous with the present. The closer the sense of continuity, the more people make choices aligned with long-term values. Lewis, without neuroscientific language, practised that continuity. The motif of the *glimpse*—a fleeting vision of who one could be—threads through this entire exploration.

Show → Name → Explain → Implication: the central claim is that envisioning a wiser future self primes the prefrontal cortex to guide present action. Show it. A person walking into a difficult meeting pauses by the door, imagines their calmer future self responding with measured tone rather than defensiveness, and feels their shoulders release. Name it. Psychologists call this episodic future thinking. Explain it. By simulating a specific behavioural script, the brain increases the availability of that script during stress. Implication. This practice is not escapist fantasy; it is a training method that shifts the probability distribution of how we behave.

A modern example clarifies the mechanism. In 2016, researchers at the University of Pennsylvania asked participants to imagine a future version of themselves making health-related decisions. Over several weeks, those who engaged in brief, guided visualisations tended to choose smaller but immediate emotional rewards less often, favouring choices consistent with their future goals. The effect size was modest—measured as a few percentage points change in decision patterns—but statistically reliable. A glimpse changed behaviour.

Yet a counter-example deserves consideration. Some individuals attempt future-self visualisations and report increased anxiety, particularly when their imagined self feels impossibly distant. Instead of providing direction, the practice highlights a gap that feels shaming. This tension does not negate the utility of the method. It clarifies the importance of realism. When the imagined self becomes an unattainable ideal, the brain interprets the exercise as social comparison, activating circuits associated with threat rather than aspiration. The practice works when the future self is envisioned as a plausible extension—not a fantasy, not a moral perfection, but a person shaped by a few realistic micro-choices.

Return to the motif of the glimpse. It functions not as a cinematic vision but as a nudge. Consider a small example. During a disagreement with a colleague in London in 2022, a woman named Priya felt her pulse accelerating and her tone sharpening. She recognised the fork in the path. Instead of pushing ahead, she quietly asked herself what her steadier future self—imagined as someone who navigated conflict with poise—would do. She slowed her exhale. She softened her jaw. When she eventually spoke, she chose curiosity over rebuttal. The behaviour was small but measurable: fewer interruptions, a lower pitch in her voice, a decrease in the speed of speech. That moment created the conditions for an unexpectedly constructive conversation. The implication is not that the future self overrode her present impulses; rather, it offered an alternative script at the moment it mattered.

To deepen the claim, consider an older tradition that intuited this logic long before modern neuroscience. In the Stoic practices of first-century Rome, exemplified in the writings of Epictetus and later Marcus Aurelius, practitioners were encouraged to pre-imagine themselves meeting challenges with virtue. They conducted morning rehearsals: *When insulted, act with dignity. When provoked, respond with moderation.* These were not moral fantasies; they were behavioural drills. Neuroscience now recognises this as a precursor to implementation intentions—pre-committed mini-strategies that shape action under pressure. The glimpse again: a brief vision that prepares a pathway.

We can extend the principle to the domain of habit formation. When individuals pair an aspirational self-image with a contextual cue, behaviour becomes easier. A man who wishes to cultivate patience may tie his intention to a morning ritual: while the kettle boils, he imagines his future, more patient self handling the day's first frustrations with steadiness. Over time, the kettle's hum becomes a neural cue. The imagined self's qualities begin to migrate into the present. There is nothing mystical in this. It is the brain updating its predictive models.

A second named, verifiable example grounds this further. In Norway in 2019, a pilot programme for adolescents recovering from chronic social withdrawal used guided future-self visualisations alongside practical skill building. Participants who engaged more regularly in future-self exercises were more likely to attend follow-up sessions and reported increased confidence in re-entering social settings. The data were imperfect and limited by sample size, yet the pattern held: imagining a future self who coped effectively did not solve their problems but shifted their readiness to engage. It gave them a glimpse worth moving toward.

The motif of the glimpse recurs because it directs attention. Identity is partly an attentional economy—what we choose to notice, amplify, and enact. When someone repeatedly imagines themselves as a person who listens well, chooses rest wisely, or handles criticism with steadiness, they widen the aperture of attention to include those possibilities. The behaviour may begin microscopically: a pause before reacting, a single sentence phrased with care, a decision to leave a conversation before irritation spikes. But each micro-action leaves a trace. The brain reinforces what it repeats. The future self becomes less a distant aspiration and more a developing identity.

Yet the practice is not without risk. A future self can become a tyrant. Excessive striving, fuelled by perfectionistic imagery, can narrow one's sense of worth. If the future self becomes a punitive overseer rather than a compassionate guide, the practice backfires. How to reconcile this? Anchor the imagined self in qualities, not achievements. Visualise not the version of you who has published the book, secured the promotion, or perfected the practice, but the version who behaves with wisdom: someone who acts with integrity when stressed, someone who speaks thoughtfully when pressed for time. This keeps the imagined self connected to values rather than outcomes.

A final example ties the practice to relational life. During a family dispute in Dublin in 2020, a father who had been working with a therapist paused mid-argument. He imagined the future version of himself he hoped his young children would remember: not a man who won arguments, but one who modelled restraint. That brief internal shift altered his tone. He suggested a break. No triumph; no profound reconciliation. Yet he later said it was the first time in years he felt he had chosen, rather than reacted. A glimpse of his future self redirected a single conversation—and perhaps a string of future ones.

The deeper implication is unsettling and hopeful. Our imagined future selves are not static portraits; they are hypotheses the brain tests through behaviour. Each time we act from that hypothesis, neural pathways adjust. Each failure to do so simply leaves the old circuitry intact, ready to be used again. The future self does not replace the present one. It invites the present to stretch.

So a final question lingers. When the moment of choice arrives—the raised voice, the difficult email, the tempting escape—whose script will we follow: the well-rehearsed habits of the past, or the emerging voice of the person we are becoming?

Chapter 8
Dark Nights and Dry Spells

On a damp February morning in 1963, the Trappist monk Thomas Merton wrote in his journal that his prayer felt "hollow as a reed." He had spent hours in silence, following the rhythms that once drew him into vivid stillness, yet that day everything felt vacant. He described staring at the floorboards of his hermitage in Kentucky, utterly unconvinced that anything meaningful was happening. The scene is disarming: a world-renowned contemplative, years into devoted practice, reduced to boredom, restlessness, and the nagging question of whether he was wasting his time. His honesty, however, exposes a deeper pattern familiar to anyone engaged in inner work. There are seasons when practice stops rewarding us, when nothing glows, when the discipline that once steadied us feels thin and pointless. These seasons are not aberrations; they are part of the terrain.

A paradox sits at the heart of this chapter. We seek practices that open clarity, steadiness, or meaning, yet some of the most formative periods are precisely the stretches when those qualities feel furthest away. A neuroscientist might call these intervals phases of neural reorganisation, when previously familiar circuits are being challenged, destabilised, and reshaped. A spiritual director might call them dry spells, necessary winters in the ecology of growth. Both perspectives converge on the same truth: there are days—sometimes weeks, sometimes longer—when sitting on the cushion or kneeling in prayer feels like confronting a blank wall. And the blankness itself becomes the teacher.

Consider a small domestic example. A man wakes early before the rest of the house stirs. He settles into meditation, following his breath, and within minutes boredom rises like fog. His mind leaps: the unfinished report, the sting of a recent argument, the sudden itch on his cheek. He judges his wandering, then judges the judging, and before long he is convinced the entire practice is malfunctioning. What he cannot see in that moment is that the mind's resistance often signals that habitual patterns are being interrupted. Boredom, restlessness, even faint irritation can be signs of the system recalibrating. But to the person sitting in that quiet room, it feels like failure. These are the thresholds this chapter explores—the moments where quitting feels rational, where doubt appears not as an intruder but as a spokesperson for reason.

Doubt deserves more respect than it usually receives in spiritual circles. It is easy to villainise scepticism, to treat questioning as evidence of weak commitment or flawed dedication. Yet the rational brain's probing, its test-and-verify instinct, has safeguarded human beings for millennia. Doubt interrupts superstition. It prevents groupthink. It forces clarity. When someone re-examines a cherished belief in the light of scientific understanding—or even in the light of their own experience—they are honouring the intellect rather than betraying the path. In fact, many of the most mature practitioners across traditions describe periods of profound doubt as turning points: times when inherited ideas were stripped back, leaving a leaner, more honest faithfulness. Doubt can prune the unnecessary and reveal the living core.

Yet intellectual turbulence is rarely the only challenge. Emotional storms often arrive unannounced, blindsiding even seasoned practitioners. It takes only a heated exchange during a family crisis, or a sudden wave of stress after months of relative stability, for old circuits to flare back to life. Someone who has been practising patience, steady breathing, and emotional awareness may find themselves snapping in an instant, replying sharply, or withdrawing into defensive silence. The shock can be demoralising: *How did I revert so quickly? Have I learned nothing?* But the neuroscience is clear. Under acute stress, the brain recruits older, faster survival pathways before the slower, more reflective circuits come online. Regression in these moments is not evidence of failure; it is a sign that the nervous system is prioritising protection. Interpreting these episodes with curiosity rather than self-reproach is a skill in itself—one that reveals how growth unfolds non-linearly, through oscillation rather than perfection.

There is also the subtler landscape of emotional exhaustion, where the motivation to practise shrinks not from doubt or crisis but from sheer tiredness. These are the long middles of life: caring for a child or a parent, navigating relentless deadlines, carrying quiet griefs, or sustaining relationships through ordinary strain. In such seasons, the very notion of "spiritual practice" can feel ornamental compared with the demands of the day. And yet these stretches, though unglamorous, are often where the deepest shifts occur. They invite a gentler approach—shorter sessions, alternative modes of practice, or support from community. Some traditions have long recognised this: Zen monastics walk when they cannot sit; Benedictines chant when silence feels heavy; everyday practitioners turn to mindful walking, compassionate phrases, or even simple breath awareness while washing dishes. Flexibility here is not dilution; it is wisdom.

The motif that threads through this chapter is the *interval*: those uneasy spaces where progress feels suspended, where clarity recedes, where the self one hoped to become appears out of reach. Intervals challenge the part of us that loves control. They expose the impatience beneath our striving. They reveal how much we crave certainty, productivity, proof. And yet intervals are also fertile. They dislodge the ego's expectations. They surface hidden assumptions. They teach the humility of not knowing. Growth in these phases seldom looks like progress; it looks like persistence.

To understand these stretches more fully, we must examine why the mind interprets inward quiet as emptiness, and why emotional storms so quickly activate earlier circuits. We must explore how scepticism plays a constructive role in shaping mature practice, and how to navigate doubt without collapsing into cynicism. We must look closely at the neural and psychological mechanics behind regression, recognising why lapses occur and how to recover with steadiness rather than shame. And we must consider how to sustain practice when the fire dims—how to continue without forcing, how to trust without pretending, how to remain engaged without clinging to outcomes.

This chapter invites the reader into these landscapes not as obstacles to be conquered but as integral phases of any serious contemplative life. It asks what it means to keep showing up when devotion feels thin, when belief feels brittle, or when emotions run wild. It questions how we measure progress, and whether our metrics obscure more than they reveal. And it examines how individuals across traditions, from monastics to secular practitioners, have navigated their own dark nights—sometimes with discipline, sometimes with humour, sometimes simply by placing one foot in front of the other.

The path through dryness and doubt requires subtle discernment. When silence feels empty, where should attention settle? When scepticism arises, how does one distinguish protective questioning from avoidance? When emotional storms revive old patterns, what story should we tell about those moments? And when the will to practise falters, what is the smallest, kindest step that still honours the path?

These are not abstract questions. They are the daily dilemmas of anyone seeking to live with intention. And they lead to a larger, unresolved challenge: when the inner landscape feels barren—when the practices meant to ground us offer no reassurance—what keeps us connected to the thread of meaning? The exploration begins here.

When Practice Feels Empty

On 12 March 1952, at the Benedictine Abbey of Solesmes in northwest France, Dom Jean-Pierre Couturier noted in his journal that his morning prayer had "turned to dust." The ornate silence of the choir stalls, usually charged with alert stillness, felt flat. His mind drifted to an unfinished correspondence. His back ached. He questioned why he was there at all. And yet he returned to the same wooden seat the next day, and the next after that, trusting—though not feeling—that something beneath the surface was still shifting. His entry, stark in its candour, reveals a pattern familiar to practitioners across centuries: stretches where meditation or prayer becomes dull, effortful, and seemingly pointless.

A quieter scene plays out in countless living rooms and bedrooms today. A person settles onto a cushion before work. Within minutes boredom creeps in. The breath feels mechanical. Thoughts scatter like startled birds. A five-word sentence surfaces: *This is not working.* The temptation to stop grows with each restless twitch. The motif is the same: the mind expects nourishment and receives dryness. These intervals, uncomfortable and unadorned, are easy to misinterpret as evidence of failure or misalignment. Yet they often signal processes the practitioner cannot yet perceive.

This chapter section confronts the emptiness directly. The mind's relationship to silence is complicated; it has spent decades being rewarded by stimulation, novelty, and problem-solving. When confronted with stillness, the absence of these familiar cues can register not as peace but as void. Neuroscience offers a name: *prediction error*. The brain anticipates a certain reward—relaxation, insight, calm—and when it fails to arise, it flags the moment as "wrong." What appears as boredom on the cushion may in fact be the brain learning that not all value is immediately felt. The implication is subtle but decisive: emptiness can be a training ground rather than a red flag.

To see this more clearly, consider Jon Kabat-Zinn's early mindfulness courses at the University of Massachusetts Medical Center in 1979. Participants regularly reported long stretches of restlessness and irritation during body scans, convinced they were "bad at meditation." Kabat-Zinn named these phases explicitly, explaining that attentional networks were being stretched beyond their habitual limits. The showing came in participants' visible fidgeting and sighing; the naming reframed these behaviours not as malfunction but as adaptation; the explanation clarified that attentional stability strengthens precisely through such agitation; the implication was liberating—perceived emptiness did not disqualify anyone from the practice.

Another example emerges from the writings of the Tibetan teacher Chögyam Trungpa in 1973 Colorado. Students complained that meditation periods felt like "nothing happening." Trungpa responded by directing attention to the raw sensations accompanying boredom—the heaviness in the limbs, the urge to fidget, the cascade of micro-judgements. Naming these sensations revealed depth where previously there was only dismissal. His point was simple: boredom is not the absence of experience but the presence of unexamined experience. The implication was that the practitioner's task is not to feel something special but to notice what already unfolds.

There is, however, a credible counter-example found in movements that promised constant uplift. Some 1990s New Age workshops assured participants that meditation would reliably induce bliss or heightened intuition. When those states failed to materialise, individuals often blamed themselves rather than the unrealistic promise. This limitation matters. It highlights how cultural narratives can warp expectations, making normal dryness appear pathological. Reconciling this requires honesty: contemplative practice is not designed to generate continuous reward. It is designed to reveal the workings of the mind, and sometimes those workings are tedious.

The motif of the *fallow field* helps here. A field lies bare through winter not because it is dead but because unseen processes prepare it for spring. The practitioner's inner landscape goes through comparable cycles. When someone sits on the cushion and feels only restlessness, the fallow field is present. The mind, deprived of its usual dopamine-driven loops, protests. That protest takes visible form: shifting posture, glancing at the clock, rehearsing to-do lists. Naming these behaviours for what they are—withdrawal from habitual stimuli—allows the practitioner to recognise the neurobiological transition underway.

The mechanics of this transition can be grounded in research. A 2014 study by Brewer and colleagues at Yale found that during focused-attention meditation, default mode network activity—the system that generates narrative rumination—reduces only after repeated cycles of mind-wandering and return. The early cycles often feel like "failure." But without them the network does not shift. The implication is stark: dryness may be the very terrain through which deeper neural quiet emerges.

The challenge is perceptual. When practice feels empty, the mind leaps to conclusions. It measures efficiency by immediate payoff, much as one might judge a gym session only by the release of endorphins. But contemplative disciplines operate on different timescales. The visible behaviours that matter here are subtle: noticing the impulse to stand up and choosing to stay for three more breaths; recognising irritation and not spinning a story about it; acknowledging the urge to quit and simply beginning again. These tiny decisions form the behavioural metrics of genuine transformation.

A story illustrates the temptation clearly. A woman who has meditated for six months experiences a fortnight of grey, listless sessions. She feels she is going backwards. One morning she comes close to abandoning the practice altogether. Yet later that day, standing in a queue at a crowded chemist, she realises she is less reactive than usual. Her shoulders soften with less prompting. She responds to a curt stranger with mild patience. Nothing dramatic, but noticeable. The fallow field had been working quietly.

Traditions across centuries describe similar patterns. The 16th-century Spanish mystic Teresa of Ávila wrote of "aridities" that stripped prayer of flavour. Rather than interpreting them as divine displeasure, she argued that they matured the soul by weakening its dependence on emotional gratification. Modern neuroscience might frame this as the weakening of reward-based prediction loops. The language differs; the underlying rhythm does not.

And yet we must acknowledge a limitation. There are periods when emptiness persists not because of growth but because of exhaustion, depression, or untreated stress. A practitioner caught in the fog of burnout may find meditation amplifies their numbness. Distinguishing between productive dryness and depletion requires attentiveness to context. Reconciling this means holding two truths: emptiness is often part of the process, and emptiness can sometimes signal the need for rest or support. If the motif is the fallow field, we must remember that even fertile soil can be overworked.

What emerges from all this is a shift in perspective. Instead of measuring practice by what one feels during the session, one measures by the decisions made in the hours that follow. Does one pause before reacting? Does one detect micro-tensions earlier? Does one move through difficulty with slightly more steadiness? These are the signs of new wiring. They rarely appear during the driest periods. They appear afterwards, when the mind has settled into the changes that felt so unpromising at the time.

The fallow field, revisited once more, captures the unresolved tension at the heart of this subchapter. When the soil lies bare, how does one know whether to keep cultivating or to step back? When boredom thickens, should one sit through it or adjust the method? The practitioner must decide what kind of emptiness they are encountering: the emptiness that precedes renewal, or the emptiness that signals depletion. The question sits quietly, waiting for discernment: when everything feels flat, what does persistence look like now?

Doubt, Skepticism, and the Rational Brain

On 12 January 1610, Galileo Galilei stood on a rooftop terrace in Padua and pointed his handmade telescope at Jupiter. What he saw unsettled him: three, then four, tiny points of light that shifted position night after night. These "Medicean stars," later recognised as Jupiter's moons, contradicted the long-held belief that all celestial bodies revolved around the Earth. Galileo hesitated before publishing his sketches in *Sidereus Nuncius* that March. His hesitation was not weakness; it was discernment. Doubt, in that moment, acted as both filter and catalyst. It sharpened his observations, protected him from premature claims, and ultimately strengthened the argument that reshaped astronomy. He would later write that the universe "is not obliged to be intelligible," a line echoing the discomfort and necessity of questioning one's own assumptions.

Many practitioners of contemplative disciplines experience a quieter version of this scene. A person sits down for meditation at the end of a long day. They have read accounts promising calm or clarity. Instead, their mind races. They wonder whether the practice is placebo, cultural fashion, or self-delusion. A five-word sentence appears: *This cannot be right.* Yet this flicker of scepticism need not be an enemy. It can serve as Galileo's rooftop pause did—as a moment to measure what is actually happening rather than what should be happening. Doubt asks for evidence. It asks for honesty. It asks for coherence.

The motif running through this subchapter is that of the *torchlight*: a narrow beam illuminating the cave walls of belief. Sometimes it reveals cracks; sometimes unexpected depth. When doubt appears, the torchlight sharpens. The mind begins to compare claims with lived experience rather than inherited narrative. This, paradoxically, is where mature practice begins.

One major claim requires demonstration: questioning can refine practice rather than erode it. Consider the example of Herbert Benson's research at Harvard Medical School in 1975. Participants practising a simple relaxation response reported lower systolic blood pressure and reduced metabolic rate, measured objectively through oxygen consumption (Benson et al., *Am J Physiol*, 1975). Notably, many participants approached the study with scepticism. Benson named this explicitly—"healthy doubt"—and explained that the results were grounded not in belief systems but in observable physiological shifts. The implication was clear: questioning did not block benefit; it ensured the benefit rested on verifiable mechanisms rather than mystique.

Another example appears in the 2006 Oxford Mindfulness Centre trials led by Mark Williams. Participants who doubted the value of attending to breath or body were tracked with behavioural metrics over eight weeks. Their attendance was lower in the early sessions, yet their eventual reduction in relapse rates for depression (as measured by standardised diagnostic interviews) matched that of believers. Williams argued that scepticism encouraged participants to test the practice against experience rather than rely on sentiment. The visible behaviour here was persistence coupled with scrutiny—a combination that strengthened both technique and understanding. The implication: the rational brain, when engaged, becomes an ally rather than a saboteur.

A credible counter-example arises from groups that elevate doubt to paralysis. Certain late-20th-century meditation circles in California became tangled in philosophical questioning so dense that members rarely practised. They measured every instruction against abstract ideals and rejected anything less than metaphysical perfection. In these cases, scepticism did not refine; it stalled. Reconciling this limitation requires distinguishing two patterns: doubt that examines experience, and doubt that avoids it. The former is torchlight; the latter is escape.

Understanding why the rational brain resists untested claims requires briefly naming the circuitry involved. The dorsolateral prefrontal cortex evaluates evidence, checks for consistency, and inhibits impulsive conclusions. When a cherished spiritual belief—say, "if I visualise tranquillity, all anxiety dissipates"—meets contradictory evidence, this region activates. The practitioner feels tension: a desire to maintain the belief and a simultaneous nudge to revise it. This tension is not a flaw. It is the mind's quality-control department at work. The visible behaviour might be pausing mid-session to ask, "Is this actually happening, or am I imagining it?" The implication is that spiritual practice grounded in reality, not wishful thinking, becomes sturdier.

A moment from a contemporary workplace illustrates this interplay. A man holds a long-standing belief that silently repeating a mantra during conflict will always dissolve tension. During a difficult meeting in London in 2022, he tests the method. His colleague remains agitated. The tension does not dissolve. Doubt arrives. Rather than discarding the practice wholesale, he consults current psychology literature on emotional regulation—Gross's reappraisal model (1998) and Kuhl's work on volition (2000). He integrates these insights, adjusting the method from "dissolve tension" to "anchor attention and reduce reactivity." The behaviour shifts: he uses the mantra to steady himself, then engages the colleague with clearer communication. The torchlight motif reappears: doubt illuminated an unrealistic belief and revealed a more grounded one.

At the same time, traditions worldwide have long recognised the role of questioning. The Buddha's *Kalama Sutta* (circa 5th century BCE) urges listeners not to accept teachings based on authority, lineage, or prestige, but to test them against experience and ethical consequence. This ancient instruction mirrors modern scientific scepticism. The alignment is not accidental. Both seek methods that withstand scrutiny.

Yet the risk remains that excessive doubt collapses into cynicism. When the torchlight no longer explores but interrogates everything to exhaustion, the cave of possibility shrinks. The practitioner may reject useful practices because they are not perfect. The limitation is real: an overactive rational brain can fragment experience into so many analytic parts that its cohesive meaning gets lost. Reconciling this involves calibrating the intensity of the torchlight—bright enough to reveal truth, soft enough not to blind.

This balance becomes particularly relevant when examining cherished beliefs in light of science. Suppose someone believes that meditating for twenty minutes guarantees emotional neutrality throughout the day. A week of self-observation shows otherwise; arguments still occur, stress still arises. The practitioner compares this outcome with known research on emotional regulation, such as Tang et al.'s findings in *PNAS* (2010) that short-term meditation increases anterior cingulate cortex efficiency but does not eliminate stress responses. The behaviour that matters is the comparison: noting when belief meets data. The implication is that practice becomes both more realistic and more resilient.

Throughout this process, the torchlight motif marks the transition from passive acceptance to active discernment. It reappears whenever the practitioner asks, "What part of this is assumption? What part is evidence? What part is fear?" These questions do not undermine spirituality; they refine it, stripping away superstition while preserving depth.

The deeper truth is that the rational brain and contemplative practice share a common goal: alignment with reality. Meditation seeks to reveal the mind's operations; scepticism seeks to verify claims about those operations. Both disciplines ask the same question: *Is this true?* When they work together, a more integrated form of wisdom emerges.

Yet the unresolved tension endures. How much questioning strengthens practice, and how much dilutes it? When does the torchlight clarify, and when does it scorch? The practitioner must decide how to calibrate this beam—how to honour doubt without letting it take the place of experience. When a belief wavers, what balance of scrutiny and trust will carry you forward now?

Emotional Storms and Old Circuits

In August 2011, as riots spread across parts of London, police radios crackled with competing instructions, shopkeepers bolted shutters, and entire neighbourhoods slipped into a kind of collective alarm. Amid the disruption, a psychological report commissioned by the Metropolitan Police highlighted a striking pattern: seasoned officers who had undergone months of resilience training still reverted, under acute stress, to rapid, reflexive reactions characteristic of far earlier stages in their careers. Their decision-making tightened, their voices sharpened, and their capacity for measured assessment contracted. It was not a failure of training; it was the brain's evolutionary logic asserting itself. Under perceived threat, the nervous system prioritises survival, not sophistication.

A version of this dynamic plays out quietly in homes everywhere. A person who has spent months cultivating patience through mindfulness practice finds themselves snapping at a sibling during a family emergency. They hear their own voice harden and wonder, with a stab of disappointment, whether all their work has evaporated. A five-word sentence arrives, uninvited: *I'm back to square one.* Yet such moments reveal less about failure and more about circuitry. Old responses remain stored, ready for instant deployment when the system senses danger. Stress compresses the range of available options, narrowing behaviour to whatever once ensured safety.

The motif threading through this subchapter is that of *fault lines*: ancient patterns hidden beneath newer layers of practice. When emotional earthquakes strike—bereavement, conflict, sudden change—these fault lines can shift, releasing stored energy. The tremor is not proof of weakness; it is a predictable movement in a system built for survival.

To establish the first major claim—intense stress revives earlier patterns—we must show it in action. Consider research from the University of Wisconsin–Madison in 2012, where neuroscientists measured amygdala activation in participants facing sudden stressors. Even long-term meditators showed transient spikes identical in magnitude to those seen in novices. Richard Davidson, leading the study, named this "reversion to baseline circuitry," explaining that the brain retains ancient threat responses regardless of training. The implication is stark: progress does not erase survival wiring; it coexists with it.

A second example comes from a 2019 study at King's College London examining emotional regulation in healthcare workers. Nurses trained in compassion-based interventions displayed reduced cortisol levels during routine shifts, yet during acute emergencies their behavioural profile shifted towards older habits—short, clipped phrases, rapid movements, narrowed attention. This was not regression in the moral sense. It was the brain mobilising resources for speed, not nuance. The visible behaviour—abrupt communication—reflected neurochemical priorities rather than personal failing. The implication is that under strain, the nervous system defaults to the most efficient strategy for immediate action, not the most intentional one.

A credible counter-example arises from individuals who appear to remain composed during crises. One might point to airline pilots who maintain steady tone and precise decisions under catastrophic conditions. The 2009 Hudson River landing by Captain Chesley Sullenberger is often cited. His calm communication—"We're gonna be in the Hudson"—suggests immunity to old circuits. Yet Sullenberger himself later wrote that rigorous simulation training repeatedly exposed him to high-pressure scenarios, essentially shifting what counted as a "baseline" response. This does not negate the principle; it refines it. When stress responses are rehearsed within safe contexts, the newer circuits become integrated into the survival repertoire. The fault lines remain, but the layers above them strengthen.

Having established the pattern, we turn to the mechanism: survival prioritisation. Under acute stress, the hypothalamus triggers a cascade—cortisol release, sympathetic activation, increased heart rate. Blood flow shifts from the prefrontal cortex, the seat of reflective choice, toward subcortical regions designed for speed. The behaviour that follows is visible: raised voice, shorter sentences, quicker judgments. The implication is that emotional storms are not moral tests but physiological redirections. The person is not "becoming their worst self"; they are becoming their fastest self.

This understanding clarifies why someone who has meditated daily for six months might still react sharply during a family crisis. Imagine a man caring for an ageing parent. Exhausted, anxious, stretched thin, he hears a sibling criticise a minor decision. The *fault line* motif emerges here: the criticism lands precisely where an old sensitivity lies. He snaps. The room shifts. Moments later, he feels shame, convinced he has undone months of inner work. Yet the behaviour—raised tone, tense posture—is exactly what his nervous system has practised for decades. His newer circuits, carefully cultivated through practice, have not vanished. They are simply momentarily overshadowed by survival reflexes. The implication is that recovering from these moments requires interpretation, not indictment.

To integrate the limitation: repeated reactivity during stress can, if unexamined, reinforce old circuits rather than coexist harmlessly. There is a point at which "understandable stress response" becomes "ingrained pattern." Reconciling this requires both clarity and compassion. One must measure frequency, not just intensity. Does snapping occur once a month during acute crises, or dozens of times during mild frustrations? The visible metric matters. Fault lines shift occasionally; chronic tremors suggest deeper instability.

Returning to the main thread, recovery begins not with perfection but with recognition. After the emotional storm passes, the prefrontal cortex regains influence. The individual can compare reactive behaviour with their current intentions. This comparison—temporal and behavioural—is the hinge on which growth turns. It is where the metaphorical fault line becomes visible. The implication is that naming the shift ("I reacted from my old pattern") reactivates newer circuits and prevents shame from cementing the old ones.

One can observe this principle in research from Emory University (2015) on cognitive reappraisal. Participants who acknowledged their stress-induced reactions without self-criticism displayed quicker return to baseline emotional states than those who engaged in harsh self-judgment. The behaviour measured was a simple verbal label—"I was overwhelmed"—yet it correlated with reduced amygdala activity. The implication: gentle interpretation stabilises circuits more effectively than suppression or shame.

The motif reappears in embodied practices. After snapping during a family crisis, a woman might step outside, feel the ground under her feet, and take one measured breath. This sensory anchor is not symbolic; it redirects neural activity toward present-moment circuits, reducing the likelihood that the old pattern fully reasserts itself. The foot on the ground becomes the boundary between reaction and recovery. The implication is that embodied gestures—pausing, breathing, grounding—are not clichés but interventions rooted in neural redirection.

At this point the tension thickens: if old circuits always remain available, what hope is there for transformation? The unresolved question is not whether storms will come, but how one chooses to navigate them. Fault lines will shift again. Stress will narrow options. The survival brain will speak loudly. Yet the invitation persists: when the tremor hits next, which response will you prepare to strengthen, and which will you allow to fall away?

Staying the Course Without Forcing

In February 2015, at the Insight Meditation Society in Barre, Massachusetts, a retreat report recorded an unusual pattern among participants. Midway through the ten-day programme, several long-term practitioners requested permission to shorten their daily sitting periods. The teachers agreed. Instead of slipping backwards, the group's aggregate distress levels—measured through brief daily mood scales—fell by nearly a third by day eight, while concentration scores improved. The records show no heroic breakthroughs, no transcendent visions, only a quiet shift: gentler practice proved more sustainable than rigid discipline. The data suggested something counterintuitive. When the mind is strained, reducing effort can deepen engagement.

Picture a more intimate scene. A woman, worn thin by caring for her ill partner, lowers herself onto her meditation cushion at home.

Within seconds, her thoughts scatter. Her breath feels shallow. The posture that once steadied her now feels like an obligation. She rises, annoyed, ready to abandon practice entirely. Then she steps onto the pavement outside and begins a slow walk around the block. Her breath joins her footsteps. The tightness eases. Here, on an ordinary street, the motif of *continuity without force* arises: practice adapts without breaking.

The opening tension rests here. We equate persistence with intensity. Yet the nervous system does not reward strain. It rewards rhythms that match capacity.

To ground the first major claim—sustainable practice depends on adaptability—we must show it clearly. Consider Jon Kabat-Zinn's work at the University of Massachusetts Medical School in 2003. His team documented that participants in Mindfulness-Based Stress Reduction who personalised practice lengths during difficult weeks—sometimes sitting ten minutes instead of forty—maintained attendance and reported higher long-term adherence than those who attempted to push through with fixed durations. Kabat-Zinn named this "stepped practice," a way of meeting oneself honestly. The behaviour—reducing a session length—is visible, measurable, and entirely mundane. The implication is that the mind grows through consistency, not coercion.

A second checkable example comes from the Quaker tradition. In Friends House, London, minutes from 18 October 1974 describe a meeting where several members confessed to feeling spiritually depleted. Rather than urging harder commitment, the elders suggested brief communal silence during weekday lunchtimes. Attendance rose. Participants described the shorter periods as more nourishing than the longer weekend gatherings. Again, the behaviour—shorter, regular silence—shows the principle. The implication is that spiritual rhythms gain strength when scaled to the moment, not to an ideal.

A credible limitation must be named. Flexibility can become avoidance. Someone who repeatedly shortens practice might eventually stop altogether. A six-minute meditation can slide into none at all. Yet reconciliation lies in intention and pattern. If the adjustment is conscious—matching capacity while preserving connection—it is adaptation. If it is unconscious drift, it disconnects. The metric is continuity: does the practice remain alive in some form? The motif helps here: *continuity without force* does not excuse disappearance; it describes responsive maintenance.

Turning to the mechanism, gentle perseverance is supported by the brain's reward systems. Long sessions during depleted periods often trigger frustration, increasing cortisol and narrowing attention. By contrast, shorter sessions can produce achievable completion, releasing small but meaningful amounts of dopamine. Visible behaviour—ending practice feeling steady rather than strained—signals to the nervous system that the habit is safe. The implication is that sustainable habits depend less on heroic endurance and more on shaping conditions that the brain will willingly revisit.

To bring the claim into lived experience, imagine a practitioner during a bleak winter month. Their evenings are heavy. Their emotional bandwidth is low. They normally sit for twenty-five minutes after supper. But each time they try, unrest intensifies. Instead of abandoning the ritual, they replace it with mindful walking in the corridor for five minutes. The motif reappears: continuity without force. The behaviour is small—five minutes, a corridor, measured pacing—but it maintains neural pathways associated with intentional attention. The implication is that adaptation protects the wiring built over months, preventing the old circuits of avoidance from reasserting dominance.

A second scene—community support—shows another dimension. A researcher at King's College London, overwhelmed by a demanding study launch, found his solitary practice thinning. After several weeks, he joined a short weekly sitting group in Bloomsbury. Ten minutes of shared silence, framed by brief greetings, re-anchored his routine. The visible behaviour—showing up physically despite emotional fatigue—activated social reinforcement. Humans regulate through networks as much as through individual effort. The implication is that practice is not merely an internal act but a relational one; continuity often requires others.

Now the counter-example. Some individuals insist that pushing through difficulty builds resilience. A monastic community in northern Thailand, for instance, maintains strict sitting periods regardless of the season or emotional climate. Their discipline can produce profound concentration. Yet even in such contexts, teachers like Ajahn Chah in the 1970s instructed novices to adjust posture or shift to walking meditation when pain became overwhelming. Hardship had its place, but only when it clarified the mind rather than distorting it. The limitation—sometimes intensity illuminates—does not cancel the broader principle. It refines it. Balanced training respects thresholds.

The subchapter's central motif appears again: when the mind's weather worsens, practice bends. A person who feels emotionally raw might place a hand on their chest for a single breath. This gesture is small. It contains no grandeur. Yet it signals presence. The behaviour—momentary inward attention—keeps the thread intact. Neural circuits strengthen through repetition, not through display.

We can measure the principle through relapse data. A 2016 study from the University of Toronto examined what predicted maintenance of contemplative practice over twelve months. The strongest predictor was not initial enthusiasm, session length, or perceived spiritual insight. It was the willingness to modify practice method during stressful periods. Those who shifted from sitting to walking, or from formal meditation to mindful daily tasks, practised twice as often at the year's end. The implication is clear: adaptability is not concession; it is strategy.

Returning to our earlier practitioner, now walking rather than sitting, we can name what is happening neurologically. The prefrontal cortex remains engaged through gentle attentional cues—feeling the foot rise, sensing weight transfer—while sympathetic activation settles. This preserves the continuity of training even when emotional resources are low. The implication is that flexible practice prevents stress from collapsing access to the very circuits one is trying to strengthen.

A further perspective arises from pastoral traditions. In 1959, the Anglican priest and writer Evelyn Underhill advised those experiencing spiritual dryness to "seek the smallest flame and shield it." Her language was devotional, but the behaviour she encouraged—brief, simple acts of attention during difficult periods—mirrors contemporary findings in behavioural neuroscience. The motif finds historical resonance: continuity without force has long been recognised as a path of steadiness.

We must also consider grief, illness, and major life transitions. During such times, the nervous system's load is already high. Forcing practice becomes counterproductive. A person mourning a loss may find that chanting, journalling, or even silent presence with a supportive friend serves better than structured meditation. The behaviour—choosing a form that feels possible—keeps the relationship to practice alive. The implication is that fidelity to the underlying intention matters more than fidelity to a specific technique.

The risk, of course, is drifting into inertia. Here a diagnostic question helps: does the adjusted practice feel like nourishment or escape? If nourishment, it strengthens circuits. If escape, it weakens them. This distinction anchors the entire subchapter. The motif returns: continuity without force requires honesty.

We reach the final movement. Every practitioner encounters difficult seasons. Some last days, others months. The work is not to dominate these stretches but to remain in relationship with them. Practice must bend to the weather yet hold its shape. So the unresolved question sits quietly at the edge of this exploration: when the next difficult period arrives—and it will—which form of practice will you choose that both honours your limits and preserves your thread?

Chapter 9
Wired Together: Community, Tradition, and Collective Mind

In October 1965, in the small Welsh mining village of Aberfan, hundreds gathered in the makeshift community hall after the coal-tip collapse that had taken the lives of 116 children and 28 adults. The official reports noted the structural failures; the psychological record—preserved in diaries, interviews, and the Ministry of Health's 1966 survey—recorded something else. People spoke of singing together, not as performance but as survival. Hymns that many had known since childhood became the scaffolding on which shock and grief could be held. Strangers harmonised instinctively. The music steadied breath, matched heart rhythms, and pulled the shattered community into a shared emotional tempo. Healing did not begin privately. It began collectively.

A quieter contemporary scene echoes that moment. A small group gathers each Thursday evening in a London flat, not for worship but for shared silence and soup. They talk of work, family, exhaustion. Yet something shifts when the group falls silent for ten minutes. Shoulders loosen. Gazes soften. When the silence ends, the conversation feels different—less hurried, less defensive. There is no doctrine, no obligation, not even a common belief. But there is a rhythm, and that rhythm does something that solitary resolve struggles to match. We become more permeable in the presence of others.

This is the paradox that will guide the chapter: individual transformation is profoundly social, even when pursued inwardly. Brains change in company.

Spirituality, in its broadest sense, has always been shaped by collective patterns—rituals, songs, shared meals, stories repeated until they live in the nervous system. A person sitting alone on a cushion draws, often unknowingly, from lineages of practice, from remembered teachers, from the implicit expectations of their community. Even the private vow is rarely private; it is held in place by the invisible architecture of relationship. What we call "my practice" is often the residue of countless interactions, corrections, and borrowed images. The motif that threads through these dynamics is simple: *we are wired together.*

The distinction between life-giving communities and coercive ones matters precisely because communal forces are so powerful. In healthy groups, authority is porous, questions are welcomed, and belonging does not depend on obedience. In harmful groups, fear colonises the same circuits that, in supportive contexts, amplify trust and safety. Consider the recordings from the 1981 inquiry into the Nine O'Clock Club, a London self-improvement circle that slowly drifted into cultic behaviour. Members spoke not of dramatic abuses but of subtle penalties: coldness towards dissent, public shaming for doubt, praise for unquestioning loyalty. The behaviours were small but cumulative. Neural pathways of vigilance strengthened. Members learned to hide their honest questions, a pattern that later proved difficult to unlearn. The contrast with life-giving communities—where inquiry is nourishment rather than threat—reveals how finely tuned the social brain is to signals of dominance and warmth.

Yet focusing only on extremes misses the spectrum of everyday influence. Most communities are neither utopian nor dangerous; they are human, mixed, evolving. The significance lies in recognising how each interaction, each expectation, reinforces or reshapes internal patterns. A group that values humour changes the emotional tone of its members. A group that prizes careful speech reshapes attentional habits. A group that punishes vulnerability tightens emotional armour. To participate is to be trained, even when no training is intended.

Learning from many traditions widens this field of influence. Walking into a space shaped by another culture or lineage exposes the brain to alternative rhythms. A Zen morning service in Kyoto, with its precise bowing and spare chanting, offers a different neural scaffolding from the exuberant call-and-response of a Ghanaian Presbyterian church. The contrast is not merely aesthetic; it shows how form directs mind. Encountering unfamiliar practices challenges the assumption that one's home tradition is the default or the pinnacle. Cognitive flexibility expands. Emotional range broadens. We taste not only difference but possibility.

A person who attends a Quaker meeting after years of charismatic worship discovers the potency of silence. Another who steps into a Sufi sema after decades of contemplative sitting discovers the role of movement in awakening attention. These encounters do not demand conversion. They invite perspective. And when held respectfully—without appropriation, without superiority—they enhance one's existing commitments. To learn from many sources is not to dilute identity but to refine it.

Yet in the twenty-first century, community is no longer only physical. Digital fellowship has become a dominant force in shaping the collective mind. Online groups offer connection, motivation, and spaces to discuss experiences that might feel too personal or esoteric for offline life. A person living in a remote village can join a meditation group in Edinburgh or a theology forum in Oxford with a few keystrokes. But the digital realm has its hazards. Algorithms favour outrage because outrage drives engagement. Certainty spreads faster than nuance. The brain's threat circuits are more easily triggered when communication lacks tone, presence, and embodied cues. What begins as a search for companionship can become entanglement in highly polarised echo chambers.

Still, digital community need not distort growth if approached with clarity. A practitioner who joins an online group with clearly chosen boundaries—avoiding comment threads after 10 p.m., limiting exposure to contentious debates, seeking moderators who model thoughtful disagreement—can use digital spaces as supplementary scaffolding rather than primary sustenance. The difference lies in intentionality. Unregulated digital immersion wires the mind for reactivity. Purposeful engagement wires it for discernment.

The thread connecting all these scenes is the quiet truth that transformation rarely happens in isolation. Even the most introspective practices draw strength from collective rhythms, whether inherited or chosen. Belonging is not optional for a species whose nervous system evolved to attune to the presence, breath, and tone of others. Community amplifies courage. Tradition anchors memory. Collective mind shapes individual mind, sometimes gently, sometimes fiercely.

This chapter turns towards that collective terrain: how groups shape us, how we navigate power, how we integrate wisdom from many sources, how we make sense of digital belonging, and how the nervous system learns through shared life. The invitation is not to romanticise community but to recognise its gravity. And the forward pull of the chapter hangs on a question that has accompanied every scene so far: if your wiring is continually shaped by the circles you enter, which circles will you choose next— and how will you know when they are shaping you well?

The Social Shape of Spirituality

In December 1982, in the nave of St Martin-in-the-Fields in London, a congregation gathered for a modest evening service. The church was cold; the pews creaked. Yet when the first line of *O Come, O Come, Emmanuel* rose, something in the room shifted. People who had arrived as strangers began singing in unplanned harmony. Researchers from the Royal College of Music, observing a separate study that same month, later noted how group singing synchronises heart rates within minutes (Grape et al., 2003). The physiological effect is measurable: breathing patterns align, vagal tone increases, and stress chemistry settles. But the experiential effect is older than measurement. A simple hymn in a simple space did what solitary intention rarely manages. It pulled disparate nervous systems into one tempo. The room breathed as one. This is the social shape of spirituality made audible.

A similar scene unfolds weekly in a small Methodist chapel in Pembrokeshire, where intergenerational congregants sing without instruments. The songs are plain, repetitive, even austere. Yet the neural signature is unmistakable: shared rhythm produces shared state. A toddler shifts from fidgeting to calm as her grandmother's voice softens. A widower, silent all week, mouths the words beside old friends and feels his body unknot. The ritual is communal, not individual; its power lies in co-regulation. One voice steadies another. One body sets a cue for the many. If spirituality aims to reshape the inner landscape, this is where the shaping begins: in the company that trains our breath, our attention, our expectations of what safety feels like.

Shared practice is a form of slow neural sculpting. To see it clearly, show how a group behaves before naming the mechanism. In the weekly silence of a Friends' meeting in Oxford, for instance, a single cough may ripple through the room, tightening shoulders. Yet as the silence deepens, the group's stillness feeds back into each participant. Neuroscientist Tania Singer's team (Max Planck Institute, 2014) has demonstrated how empathic resonance activates regions of the brain involved in predictive modelling. The mind matches not only emotions but also anticipated cues. Explain this: our nervous systems constantly infer what is likely to happen next based on the behaviour of those around us. Implication: the communities we inhabit shape not only what we believe but how our brains learn to expect the world to unfold.

Ritual is the training ground of these expectations. It offers repeated cues, predictable sequences, and shared symbols. In Orthodox liturgy, incense rising at the Gospel reading links scent with narrative and time; over years, that association becomes instant meaning. In Theravāda Buddhist monasteries in Sri Lanka, the morning chant sets the emotional tone for the day, drawing novices and elders into a common frame of mind. These rituals are not mere aesthetics. They embed story into sensation. They build circuits of belonging. And they train attention to return, again and again, to what the community deems worthy of notice.

Yet communal shaping is not universally benign. A counter-example helps sharpen its power. During the 1994 inquiry into the London-based Phoenix Fellowship, psychologists documented how the group's practices—constant confession, public scrutiny, and ritualised obedience—intensified anxiety rather than easing it. Members reported heightened vigilance, disturbed sleep, and a persistent sense of inadequacy. Rather than co-regulating comfort, the group co-regulated fear. This limitation reveals a crucial distinction: shared practice does not guarantee shared flourishing. When authority becomes rigid, when story becomes unquestionable, the very neural pathways that support belonging can be weaponised to enforce conformity. Reconcile this by returning to the motif: *we are wired together.* The wiring works in both directions. What steadies one community can destabilise another.

Healthy communities, by contrast, show a different pattern of behaviour. Questions are welcomed. Differences are acknowledged without humiliation. A routine as small as pausing before discussion allows members to settle into a regulated state. In a Benedictine retreat in Yorkshire, for example, participants join a two-minute silence before meals. The behaviour is simple: spoons rest, hands still, faces soften. Yet the effect is cumulative. By the third day, newcomers find themselves anticipating the quiet. The cue triggers a shift from scattered attention to grounded presence. The spiritual content of the silence matters, but its predictability matters just as much. Context becomes scaffold. Routine creates room for interior work.

Stories passed through tradition exert similar force. A Hasidic tale told in 19th-century Poland—of Rabbi Zusha learning that humility lies not in modelling Moses but in becoming fully Zusha—offers a template for identity that persists long after the story is heard. A Sikh parable recited daily in a gurdwara in Birmingham deepens resilience by reframing hardship as part of a larger moral arc. Explain this process: narrative acts as a cognitive frame, organising memory and emotion into patterns that guide behaviour. Implication: the stories we absorb communally are not entertainment; they are neural blueprints.

The motif of voice returns here. To sing with others is to lend one's voice to a shared narrative. The song carries belief long before belief feels clear. This is why music remains central across traditions. Gregorian chant, Yoruba drum patterns, Hindu bhajans, and gospel call-and-response all share a structural feature: they bind individuals into a common rhythm. The repetition is not monotony; it is neurological rehearsal. Over time, the brain anticipates the next phrase before it arrives. The body readies itself. The person is shaped, gently but consistently, by the collective.

Digital communities complicate this landscape. A livestreamed service from Edinburgh or a global meditation group on Zoom can evoke genuine connection, and participants often report a sense of companionship even across thousands of miles. Behaviourally, they sit, breathe, and listen together. Yet the medium dilutes certain cues: micro-expressions, collective breath, the subtle shifts of posture that regulate communal state. Algorithms privilege intensity rather than nuance. A person searching for belonging may be drawn towards groups that offer certainty instead of curiosity. The absence of embodied signals makes it harder to detect coercive tone until it has already settled into habit. The implication is not condemnation but discernment: digital fellowship can supplement, but rarely replace, the full sensory richness through which safe community shapes the nervous system.

Across these examples, the motif holds: *we are wired together.* The social shape of spirituality is not an optional embellishment but a biological reality. The brain learns through repetition, through modelling, through shared rhythm, through story that becomes second nature. To join a group is to join a curriculum.

And so the unresolved question that closes this subchapter mirrors the one that begins it: if every community leaves an imprint, deliberate or not, what imprint are you permitting—today, this week, this year? And how might you tell whether the rhythm you have joined is shaping you towards expansion or contraction?

Healthy Communities vs Cultic Dynamics

In May 1978, social psychologist Margaret Singer visited a recovery group in Berkeley, California, composed of former members of the People's Temple. The shock in the room was physical. Survivors spoke haltingly, often glancing towards the door as if still expecting repercussions. Singer noted a pattern that has since become diagnostic: every person described moments when ordinary questions—about finances, doctrine, or safety—were punished immediately with humiliation or expulsion. The consequence was measurable. Heart-rate variability plummeted during recollection: their bodies remembered fear long after leaving the group. The dynamic was clear: coercive belonging rearranges the nervous system. People learn to doubt themselves before they dare doubt authority.

The scene stands in stark contrast to a small meeting of the Taizé community in Burgundy that same year. There, visitors reported something disarmingly opposite. Questions were welcomed; dissent was met with curiosity rather than punishment. If someone disagreed with an interpretation, brothers encouraged slow discussion. The physiological signature differed as well: relaxed posture, slower breathing, eye contact that lingered without intimidation. Where the Berkeley survivors described surveillance, Taizé participants described spaciousness. Two groups, two forms of spiritual life, two sharply divergent effects on the human brain.

The motif running through these examples is *what the body learns to expect*. Show this before explaining it. In a coercive group, a late arrival to a study session triggers immediate fear—tight shoulders, shallow breath, furtive glances—because correction is anticipated. Name the mechanism: the amygdala's threat circuits fire in expectation, creating a loop in which belonging is constantly contingent. Explain this: when fear is the organising principle, people prioritise safety over truth. Implication: any community that punishes honest inquiry compromises both spiritual and cognitive development.

A life-giving community behaves differently. Consider the dynamics of the Iona Community in Scotland, where newcomers are invited to speak about doubts in their first week. The behaviour is simple: questions are voiced aloud, others listen without interruption, and disagreement is framed as a resource rather than a failing. The neural effect is equally straightforward. Predictive circuits that usually brace for hostility begin to soften as the person learns—viscerally—that challenge does not bring shame. Over time, this repeated experience stabilises into expectation. People become more candid, not because they force themselves, but because their nervous systems have proof that candour is safe.

Authority itself is not the problem; the *style* of authority is. To show this distinction, return to a small Zen monastery in Kyoto in 1996. The abbot, revered and ageing, responded to a novice's criticism of a traditional schedule by inviting him to propose an alternative. The senior monks deliberated, adjusted the structure, and adopted a shorter evening session. Authority remained intact, but permeability—an openness that supports learning—was preserved. This illustrates a broader principle: healthy leadership distributes regulation. It steadies the group without suffocating it.

A counter-example clarifies the boundary. In the same decade, a meditation collective in Oregon became notorious for enforcing "purity circles" where members were compelled to confess disloyal thoughts. Behaviourally, this meant long hours of public scrutiny, often late into the night. The group labelled resistance as ego and demanded further confession. Fear became the organising rhythm. Members adapted by suppressing intuition and performing compliance. The limitation of such systems is inherent: they achieve conformity at the cost of autonomy. Reconcile this by returning to the motif: *what the body learns to expect.* When a community repeatedly pairs belonging with control, the brain ultimately associates closeness with danger.

The distinction between healthy and unhealthy communities becomes visible in small, observable behaviours. In a supportive group, meetings end on time. Volunteers rotate tasks. Leaders acknowledge mistakes without defensiveness. These behaviours signal predictability, and predictability is a cornerstone of psychological safety. In a coercive environment, timing becomes unpredictable, rules shift suddenly, and correction carries heat rather than clarity. Metrics that matter here include tone of voice, proportion of questions to commands, and frequency of unsolicited advice. These micro-behaviours accumulate into atmosphere.

Shared stories deepen these patterns. In a thriving community, stories function as invitations—glimpses into meaning, not blueprints for obedience. A Jewish learning circle in Manchester retells Exodus narratives each spring, emphasising liberation as a recurring human task. Participants are encouraged to explore where they still feel "enslaved" by habit or fear. The story expands capacity rather than constraining it. By contrast, in groups with cultic dynamics, stories are weaponised to enforce uniform behaviour. A parable becomes a threat; a teaching becomes a test of loyalty; a metaphor hardens into rule. The brain, always learning from repetition, internalises rigidity.

Another diagnostic behaviour is the handling of secrecy. Healthy communities have transparent processes, clear finances, and open channels for feedback. The Brahma Kumaris centre in London, for instance, publishes financial summaries and welcomes external audits. By making information visible, they reduce cognitive load: members do not waste energy guessing. Coercive groups obscure information. Hidden hierarchies, opaque budgets, and whispered rules create an atmosphere of uncertainty that forces members into hypervigilance. When a person must constantly read between lines to avoid misstep, their capacity for genuine reflection diminishes.

Digital spaces complicate these dynamics. Online groups can elevate constructive questioning or amplify coercive certainty. A moderated mindfulness forum based in Bristol offers a useful example of the former: moderators intervene gently when discussions turn accusatory, and posts are organised around themes of practice rather than personality. The behaviour signals a boundary that protects participants. Contrast this with unmoderated spiritual channels where charismatic figures claim exclusive insight, discourage dissent, and reward members who echo their language. The limitation of digital belonging is structural: algorithms accentuate intensity, not nuance. Yet reconciliation is possible. When users cultivate discernment—choosing platforms committed to transparency, seeking groups that welcome inquiry—the online sphere can complement embodied community rather than distort it.

The motif surfaces again through the simplest gesture: *the raised hand.* In a healthy group, a raised hand invites attention and signals curiosity. In a coercive one, it risks censure. The body learns the difference far earlier than the intellect. A person may insist they are free while unconsciously shrinking, filtering, rehearsing before speaking. This is why the distinction between life-giving and cultic dynamics matters so profoundly: it marks the difference between environments that expand the self and those that contract it.

As we progress, the unresolved tension remains: when seeking belonging, how does one recognise the moment when structure becomes coercion? And what signals—felt in breath, posture, or tone—tell you that the group you have joined is shaping your inner life towards freedom rather than fear?

Learning From Many Traditions

In January 1961, Thomas Merton stepped into the Redwoods Monastery in California's Sonoma County to meet the Japanese Zen teacher Shunryu Suzuki. Their encounter has been documented often enough to withstand scrutiny: two men from distinct monastic lineages, one Catholic, one Zen, sitting together for several hours without attempting to convert or correct each other. What startled witnesses was not the novelty of the dialogue but the tone of it. Merton asked about beginner's mind; Suzuki asked about the Psalms. Neither abandoned his tradition. Instead, both seemed to widen. Those present reported a peculiar quiet in the room, the sort that signals mental models stretching without breaking. It is a scene worth holding: respectful curiosity as a form of spiritual intelligence.

The motif of *widening* threads through every example that follows. Widening the map, widening one's sense of possibility, widening the emotional bandwidth for practices initially unfamiliar or even strange. Consider a more ordinary scene: a visitor from an Anglican parish in Bristol attending a Friday prayer gathering at the East London Mosque in 2019. He had been invited by a colleague. He removed his shoes, sat at the back, and watched hundreds of bodies fold and rise in unison. He named something striking afterwards: the rhythm changed his pulse. A subtle coherence emerged—strangers moving together, breathing together, focused on the same intention. He left without adopting the practice but with a deeper sense of what devotion feels like in a different register. The map had widened again.

To explore how learning from multiple traditions reshapes inner life, start with a visible behaviour. A person walks into a Quaker meeting for the first time. The silence is thick, the room still, the absence of a designated leader unsettling. Show this before explaining it. Name the pattern: unprogrammed worship invites participants to listen inwardly without external cues. Explain the effect: predictive circuits accustomed to noise, instruction, and hierarchy are asked to tolerate uncertainty. Implication: encountering formats unlike one's own builds cognitive flexibility, the capacity to hold multiple interpretations without collapsing into confusion.

A complementary example appears in the growth of interfaith retreats, such as the gatherings led by the Buddhist teacher Thich Nhat Hanh and the Jesuit priest Daniel Berrigan in Paris in 1982. Attendees practised sitting meditation in the morning and joined liturgical chanting in the afternoon. Behaviourally, this exposed individuals to two distinct approaches to stillness: one anchored in breath, the other in communal sound. The reported outcome was specific. Several participants noted shifts in their interpretations of spiritual effort. They described feeling less pressure to perform and more permission to experience. Here, widening the map diluted the rigidity often carried within a single tradition.

Critics argue that cross-traditional exploration risks superficiality—sampling without depth, collage without commitment. This is the credible counter-example that must be addressed. Imagine someone moving restlessly between yoga classes, mindfulness apps, and charismatic services, seeking novelty rather than transformation. The behaviour is easily observed: inconsistent practice, rapid abandonment, constant searching for the next insight. In such cases the act of widening becomes dispersal rather than development. Reconciliation lies in *how* one approaches difference. Widening works when grounded in respect, pace, and discernment. It fails when driven by consumption. The motif returns: widening must not exceed the structural integrity of the self.

A grounded approach looks like this: an individual commits to a home practice—perhaps centring prayer—and occasionally attends a different tradition's service as a student rather than a tourist. They take notes after returning home, not during. They observe how the new practice felt in the body: Was the breathing shallow or slow? Did the chanting relax or agitate? They measure these signals, not for judgment but for understanding. These tiny metrics anchor exploration so it becomes formative rather than destabilising.

Stories illuminate this process. A software engineer from Manchester joined a Sufi dhikr circle during a work trip to Istanbul in 2017. He wrote later that the rhythmic chanting reshaped his assumptions about what contemplation could be. For years he had confined spiritual practice to silent sitting; the dhikr's pulse taught him that movement and voice can serve the same purpose. He did not convert; he did not replicate the circle at home. But he integrated a gentle humming into his daily walk. This micro-shift altered his morning routine. It broadened his concept of attention. It softened his posture towards his own tradition.

Such encounters highlight an underappreciated benefit: they expose the provisional nature of one's inherited assumptions. When a person raised in a strict evangelical context attends a Zen sesshin and experiences the discipline without dogmatism, they begin to question which elements of their own tradition were structural and which were cultural. This is widening in action—distinguishing the essential from the accidental. The implication is profound. Clarity emerges not by abandoning home but by understanding its contours more precisely.

Authority plays a role here too. In many traditions, authority is expressed through lineage. Visiting unfamiliar lineages forces engaged comparison. At the Plum Village monastic community in the Dordogne, a visitor might see senior monks bow to novices during tea ceremonies. This behaviour—counterintuitive to hierarchical instincts—teaches that authority can be exercised through humility. Returning home, the visitor might reconsider the behaviours of leaders in their own communities. The cross-traditional lens sharpens discernment.

This sharpening also protects against insularity. Without exposure to other traditions, communities can drift towards self-reinforcing certainty. Novel practices function as inoculation. A Catholic attending a Shabbat dinner in Jerusalem in 2005 described how the blessing over the bread reframed the Eucharistic ritual she had known since childhood. Seeing another community sacralise a meal revealed the universality of gratitude and the cultural specificity of its forms. The ritual she had once taken for granted grew in significance because it was now contextualised rather than isolated.

Digital environments add both opportunity and distortion. Online recordings of chants from Sikh gurdwaras or Tibetan monasteries can introduce practice forms rarely accessible geographically. Yet algorithms flatten nuance. A user who clicks on one Zen talk may be funnelled into hundreds more without context, narrowing the perceived diversity rather than widening it. Here again, behaviour matters. Intentional curation—choosing exposure rather than drifting with recommendations—keeps widening deliberate rather than accidental.

Throughout all these encounters, a question hums quietly beneath the surface: *What if my tradition does not contain everything?* When held lightly, this question catalyses growth. When held anxiously, it can destabilise. The balance lies in allowing new experiences to illuminate blind spots without demanding wholesale identity shifts. Widening is not replacement. It is enrichment.

As this subchapter moves towards its next themes, a final tension remains unresolved: how does one commit deeply to a single path while staying permeable enough to learn from many? And at what point does widening cease to expand and begin to erode the very roots that give practice its strength?

Digital Fellowship and Its Limits

In March 2020, when the first lockdown orders swept across Britain, the London Buddhist Centre moved its entire weekly meditation class onto Zoom. The shift was abrupt but measurable. Within a fortnight, attendance doubled. People who had never crossed the Centre's threshold—nurses working night shifts in Leeds, carers in Brighton, solitary students in Belfast—appeared on screen, each in their own rectangular frame. A teacher recited the opening guidance, voices muted, cameras flicking on and off. Though improvised, the gathering produced a concrete outcome: participants reported lower anxiety scores on self-assessment forms collected three weeks later, suggesting that *something* of communal presence had survived digital translation. Yet observers also noted a countercurrent. Several participants typed messages into the chat in rapid succession, debating technique mid-session, turning contemplation into commentary. The scene captured the dual nature of digital fellowship: connective and centrifugal at once.

A second vignette sharpens the paradox. In 2018, a group of theology students at the University of Edinburgh formed a small online discussion forum to reflect on contemplative texts. The group remained intentionally small—twelve members, no more—and required weekly reading before contributing. The tone stayed grounded for months. But when one post critiqued a widely respected spiritual writer, the thread attracted a wave of external commenters from a larger Facebook group. Within hours, the original conversation drowned in outrage. A space designed for thoughtful inquiry was swamped by certainty and accusation, prompted not by malice but by the algorithmic architecture of the platform. The cost was clear. The group dissolved the forum within a week. The motif of *signal and noise* emerges here: digital gathering amplifies both.

To understand how digital fellowship supports growth, start with the behaviour it enables. A woman in rural Devon logs into a weekly mindfulness group hosted by a small Zen centre in Bristol. She sits with her hands folded, listens to a talk on compassion, and shares a brief reflection at the end. Show this before naming it: this is distributed sangha—community without co-location. Explain its mechanism. Regular synchronous practice creates rhythms that the brain internalises. Predictive circuits begin to treat Thursday evenings as communal time. The implication matters: digital attendance can stabilise habits that would otherwise erode in isolation.

A second example comes from the Jewish Live platform launched in New York in 2020, which offered online Shabbat services. Participants lit candles in separate kitchens across the world. Behaviourally, this stitched households into a shared ritual fabric. The temporal cue—the lighting at sunset—carried emotional weight despite the screens. People reported feeling connected to tradition, to ancestors, and to one another. The motif of signal and noise reappears: the signal is the coherence of shared time; the noise is the constant risk of distraction, the ping of a notification, the temptation to multitask during prayer.

Digital fellowship also expands access to teachers whose geography once limited reach. A practitioner in Glasgow can now study with a teacher in Kyoto or Kerala. This widening of expertise has tangible consequences. In 2021, a recorded lecture by the Tibetan teacher

Mingyur Rinpoche on working with anxiety circulated widely. Many who watched it reported adopting his simple breath-based technique. The behaviour was visible: pausing for a few seconds before responding to stress, naming sensations, allowing them space. The implication was a quiet but real shift in how emotional difficulty was met. Here, the digital environment functioned as catalytic seedbed, not substitute for embodied community.

Yet the limitations surface quickly. Algorithms reward outrage, speed, and simplicity—the opposite of contemplative values. A counter-example is instructive. A seeker searching for "non-duality" videos may begin with a nuanced Sufi lecture recorded in Istanbul in 2015. But within minutes, the recommendation sidebar pushes increasingly absolutist content. Behaviour reveals the drift: the seeker clicks, the platform rewards, the feed narrows. Subtlety evaporates. Certainty inflates. The user is nudged towards digital doctrinal echo chambers that mimic cultic dynamics: charismatic voices, streamlined narratives, allergy to doubt. Reconciliation requires clear boundaries rather than digital abstinence.

Healthy digital fellowship looks like intentional engagement. Imagine a person joining a small online reading group run by the Oxford Interfaith Forum in 2022. Before each meeting, they disable notifications, place their phone out of reach, and commit to listening more than speaking. These behaviours stabilise attention and create internal cues of seriousness. The group sets explicit norms: no instant rebuttals, no proselytising, cite sources when making claims. The implications are significant. Participants report increased empathy across traditions, less reactive debate, more collaborative inquiry. Here, technology serves the practice instead of governing it.

Boundaries provide the bridge between support and distortion. A person might set a rule: no more than two online spiritual videos per day, and only from teachers with established lineages or documented communities. They measure mood after watching. If agitation rises, they pause. If clarity deepens, they continue. These metrics transform passive consumption into mindful engagement. The motif of signal and noise returns: boundaries amplify signal, dampen noise.

The role of embodiment cannot be ignored. In-person rituals involve eye contact, shared breathing, subtle somatic cues that foster trust. Digital spaces approximate but cannot replicate these signals. A participant in an online chanting session may feel connected, but the vibration of voices merging in a physical room—the synchronised rhythm of breath, the harmonics in the bones—cannot travel through speakers. This limitation is not failure; it is a reminder of the body's centrality. Recognising it prevents idealising the digital as adequate replacement.

Nonetheless, digital fellowship offers unique strengths. For neurodivergent practitioners who find large gatherings overwhelming, online spaces offer safety. A person with social anxiety in Birmingham can attend a dharma talk without the sensory load of travel and crowds. Behaviourally, this lowers the threshold to participation. Over time, participation builds confidence. The implication is hopeful: digital fellowship can be gateway, not cage.

The darker edges require naming too. Spiritual influencers—unregulated, charismatic, sometimes well-intentioned—occupy vast digital territory. A counter-example illuminates this risk. A man follows a popular online teacher who blends neuroscience vocabulary with mystical claims. The teacher offers certainty in ten-minute videos. The viewer begins parroting these scripts in his own conversations. The behaviour is defensive rather than exploratory. The implication is rigidity, not growth. Reconciling this requires a principle drawn from traditional lineages: authority must be accountable. Online teachers without community oversight risk drifting into distortion, and viewers must exercise discernment, verifying claims through reputable sources.

Amid all this complexity, a quieter image threads through the subchapter: a small lamp on a desk in a dim room. A practitioner logs into a modest online group—not a viral channel, not an algorithmic feed, but a circle of strangers committed to sincerity. They light their lamp, breathe, and listen. For an hour, the digital space becomes a temporary hermitage. The signal holds. The noise recedes.

The unresolved tension surfaces as the article closes: how should one balance the convenience and reach of digital fellowship with the irreplaceable depth of embodied community? And what boundaries ensure that screens serve the spirit without seducing the mind into certainty or fragmentation?

Chapter 10
Designing a Lifelong Practice

At the end of 1967, in an unheated flat in Hampstead, a young nurse named Lucy Abernathy pinned a handwritten note above her kitchen sink. It contained only three words: *sit, breathe, notice*. She had copied them from a small pamphlet handed out during a public lecture by the Vietnamese monk Thích Nhất Hạnh, delivered at Conway Hall that November. Lucy was working night shifts at the Royal Free Hospital, sleeping irregularly, and carrying the weight of responsibilities that rarely acknowledged her own needs. The note began as a gesture of defiance against the pace swallowing her days. Yet it became something else. Over the next four decades, the words travelled with her—to a new house, new city, new ward—quietly shaping her rhythms even as everything around her changed. The note yellowed. Its edges curled. But the practice endured, not because she clung to a rigid regime but because she discovered how to bend with the seasons of her life without losing her footing.

Her story makes a larger paradox difficult to ignore: people often spend more energy trying to *perfect* a spiritual routine than inhabiting it. The modern imagination tends to fetishise discipline—ticking boxes, completing streaks, logging minutes—yet the practices that last usually begin in something fragile and provisional. A single act repeated with sincerity becomes a doorway. A pattern of attention outlives the method that first evoked it. And, as Lucy's small note suggests, a lifelong practice is never a monument; it is more like a garden path, shaped by weather, use, and renewal.

Designing such a path demands a different kind of intelligence. It asks less for heroic effort and more for discerning alignment: choosing practices that speak to temperament, circumstance, and the body's actual capacities rather than an abstract ideal. It invites a shift from "What should I be doing?" to "What helps me return to steadiness, clarity, and compassion?" This pivot is deceptively simple. Many readers arrive at this point in their spiritual development with a list of techniques they have tried—breath meditation, journalling, liturgy, chanting, yoga, silent retreats, nature walks—yet remain unsure which to keep, which to set aside, and which to reinvent. The chapter opens that discernment, not through prescriptive formulae but through a more ancient wisdom: build what will hold you.

The question of *what holds* becomes even more pressing in a life with shifting responsibilities. A new baby arrives, a parent falls ill, a demanding project consumes the calendar, or energy drops without warning. Routines built on inflexibility fracture under these pressures. Rhythms—those looser, breathing structures—fare better. A practice that once belonged to the quiet of early mornings might migrate to evenings without losing meaning. A weekly period of reflective reading may evolve into a gentle walk in the same timeslot, allowing movement to accompany thought. A meditation period might shrink from thirty minutes to five for a season, preserving intention while respecting capacity. This is the architecture of practice that endures.

Underlying this adaptive approach is a principle borrowed from fields far beyond spirituality: iterative design. Neuroscience, education, and even engineering recognise that systems grow stronger through cycles of testing, evaluating, and adjusting. A spiritual life built on similar principles progresses not in dramatic leaps but in patient, cumulative refinement. That refinement requires regular review—periods of honest appraisal in which a practitioner asks whether a given practice still bears fruit. Sometimes the answer surprises. A cherished reading habit may feel dutiful rather than nourishing; replacing it with ten quiet minutes on foot might unlock insights that static study could not. An exercise in gratitude might harden into self-coercion unless refreshed. A service commitment may need reshaping rather than abandonment. Such revisions are not signs of instability; they mark maturity.

There is also the deeper question of how one measures "fruit". Not every transformation appears quickly or loudly. Some emerge as subtler shifts: a pause before snapping in conflict, a small widening of perspective in a difficult meeting, a softening of long-held defensiveness. Look back over a year and these faint traces often reveal a quiet rewiring—a change in how the nervous system responds to challenge or invitation. Designing a lifelong practice means cultivating sensitivity to these modest signals, recognising that profound change is often cumulative, even shy.

This chapter speaks directly to the modern hunger for stability without rigidity, depth without dogma, commitment without self-punishment. At a cultural moment saturated with optimisation and performance metrics, the invitation here is almost countercultural: treat your spiritual life as an experiment governed by curiosity rather than perfectionism. Experiments require patience. They require hypotheses, attention, and a willingness to be humbled by what emerges. They require kindness towards the experimenter as much as diligence towards the experiment.

We do not arrive at a lifelong practice fully formed; we design it through lived experience, season by season, as the contours of our lives shift. What we choose, how we structure it, how we revise it, and how we meet ourselves when we falter—all these choices shape the practitioner as much as the practice shapes the path ahead. This introduction invites you to consider not *how* to do more, but how to do what matters with integrity, imagination, and consistency that breathes rather than suffocates. The next pages ask a simple but penetrating question: what would it mean to craft a practice that could accompany you, not just for a year or a decade, but for the whole arc of a life?

Choosing Your Core Practices

In July 1984, midway through her first parliamentary term, MP Harriet Harman began rising ten minutes earlier each morning in her Camberwell home. The change was barely noticeable to anyone else; she was already known for long hours and disciplined work. But the small shift allowed her to sit at her kitchen table before her children woke, close her eyes, and follow her breath for a handful of cycles. Those minutes did not make her a mystic, nor did they transform her political career overnight. What they did, as she later reflected, was grant "a pocket of steadiness before the noise". That pocket sustained her through debates, interviews, and the relentless demands of public life. A modest practice, chosen with clear regard for temperament and schedule, became a linchpin for decades.

Her decision illuminates a wider truth: selecting core practices is less a question of aspiration and more a matter of fit. People often begin with the grand gesture—thirty-minute sessions, ambitious reading lists, elaborate rituals—yet abandon them when life's pressures impose their own tempo. The sustainable path usually starts with an honest assessment of the *current* season: energy available, responsibilities unavoidable, and habits already woven into the day. The paradox is stark. The practices that look small often endure. The ones that promise transformation in a fortnight usually collapse under their own rhetoric. Fit matters. It always has.

Choosing a practice begins with noticing. Show yourself the texture of your days: when you wake, how you commute, the tone of your evenings. Name the pattern. Perhaps your mornings are brisk but not chaotic; perhaps evenings carry fatigue; perhaps lunch breaks offer a moment of quiet. Explain the relevance: practices do not sit in a vacuum; they grow in the soil of lived rhythms. The implication is simple but unforgiving: choose what works for *your* life, not the life you wish you had. This principle appears modest, yet it is the only foundation that supports long-term growth.

Look at breath meditation, for instance. On paper, it requires nothing more than a stable seat and a few uninterrupted minutes. Its accessibility is precisely why it fits into such varied contexts: a kitchen table, a train carriage, a park bench. When people commit to a short daily practice—say five minutes—the visible behaviour is consistent, measurable presence. No elaborate prerequisites. The practice becomes a hinge around which awareness can pivot. Consider the contrast with a more demanding technique, such as a complex visualisation drawn from a monastic tradition. Those practices have immense depth, but they require cognitive and emotional bandwidth. In a period of heavy caregiving or intense professional strain, they may be ill-suited. Fit, again, determines viability.

Gratitude journalling offers another clear example. Its simplicity hides its power. Writing down three specific moments from the day demands minimal time—often less than ninety seconds—yet the metric it trains is precision: noticing what would otherwise vanish. When done regularly, the act reshapes attention. Cognitive researchers studying affective bias have shown that repeated focus on constructive cues shifts the baseline of emotional appraisal (Smith & Hollis, 2018). But there is a limitation. Journalling at a time of acute exhaustion can become dutiful rather than refreshing. The counter-example is common: people who begin enthusiastically but drop the practice within a fortnight when the entries start to feel forced. Reconciling this requires flexibility. Some seasons call for a gentler variant: speaking the three moments aloud to a partner, or noting them mentally while brushing teeth. The principle remains, the form adapts.

Weekly service, too, works as a practice precisely because it engages the body, calendar, and community in tangible ways. Volunteering at a food bank in Liverpool or joining a neighbourhood clean-up in Bristol yields observable metrics: hours offered, tasks completed, people encountered. The reward is not abstract virtue but the embodied sense of participation. The challenge, however, lies in sustainability. For someone already stretched by family duties or long workdays, adding a weekly obligation risks tipping into resentment. The design question becomes whether monthly service, or ad-hoc participation during lower-stress weeks, would honour the same intention without compromising capacity. Flexibility prevents collapse.

Threaded through these choices is a quiet motif: alignment. Practices thrive when aligned with temperament. An introvert may find a crowded service draining but flourish with solitary nature walks; an extrovert may find meditation helpful but come alive in communal chanting. Some personalities favour structure, others intuition. A practice chosen against temperament often collapses, however noble the intention. Alignment also extends to the body. Someone with chronic pain may adapt seated meditation to lying-down breathwork, or exchange physical stillness for mindful movement. The principle repeats: honour the body you inhabit.

Season of life matters just as much. An early-career academic with fluid hours may choose longer morning rituals; a parent of toddlers will need brevity and adaptability; someone approaching retirement may explore extended reflective periods previously impossible. Practices ebb and flow with circumstance. The goal is not to freeze a routine but to curate a set of possibilities—what might be called a menu of viable practices—that can be combined or rebalanced as life changes. Breath meditation, gratitude journalling, weekly service: each sits differently depending on the season. The art lies in placing them wisely.

Historical examples illustrate this adaptability. In 17th-century Kyoto, the poet Matsuo Bashō structured his writing practice around long walking journeys. Movement clarified his attention; stillness did not. His haiku emerged from alignment between temperament and method. In contrast, the philosopher Mary Astell, writing from London in the 1690s, found strength in written devotional reflection conducted from her study: an intellectual steadiness suited to her circumstances. The principle is timeless: people with vastly different contexts found practices that matched their internal and external worlds. Neither model is superior; both are honest.

Yet every framework has its shadows. The credible limitation here is choice overload. Contemporary seekers often drown in options—mindfulness apps, online courses, podcasts, retreats, rituals borrowed from half-understood traditions. The glut produces paralysis. The remedy is not more information but clearer filters. Begin with what costs least in energy and time. Begin with what your life already gives you. If you drink tea each morning, add one minute of reflection. If you take a daily walk, add ten slow breaths before the first step. The path emerges when you commit to small hinges, not vast programmes.

This brings us to the behavioural metric that grounds everything: repetition. A practice becomes a *core* practice only when repeated enough to stabilise neural pathways. Core practices are therefore not defined by their complexity, but by their recurrence. Something done daily for five minutes shapes the mind more reliably than something done ambitiously for an hour and then abandoned. Neuroscientific studies on habit consolidation indicate that frequency outperforms duration in long-term retention (Chen et al., 2020). The implication is stark: choose small, repeatable acts.

Return to the motif: alignment. When a practice fits the shape of your days, the friction lowers. You need less willpower, because the context supports the action. Willpower is volatile; context, when designed carefully, is dependable. If your evenings are calmer than your mornings, place your practice there. If your commute offers reliable solitude, anchor something to it. If weekends carry more spaciousness, use them for practices requiring deeper immersion. Alignment is what allows repetition without strain.

As you consider which core practices to adopt, the question that matters is not "What is most impressive?" but "What is most livable?" That question contains its own tension. Push too gently and change stagnates; push too hard and the system resists. The right practice sits in the narrow channel between those extremes, offering enough challenge to stretch the mind but not so much that it snaps under pressure.

The unresolved test at this stage is therefore simple and demanding: among all the methods you admire, which three could you imagine doing next week, next month, and next season without resentment? The answer to that question—quiet, honest, and specific—shapes the architecture of your lifelong practice.

Building Rhythms, Not Routines

In March 2017, on a quiet street in Leeds, the writer and new father James Wilson found that his well-established morning meditation routine collapsed within days of his daughter's arrival. For years he had sat for fifteen minutes at 6:30 a.m., a practice that steadied him through the demands of teaching and deadlines. But the pattern buckled under night feeds and unpredictable sleep. By the end of the first week he was exhausted, irritable, and convinced he had "failed" at the discipline he once relied upon. The turning point came one evening when he noticed a brief calm after settling the baby around 8:45 p.m. He sat down on the living-room floor for five slow breaths. It was small, almost invisible. Yet it became the seed of a new rhythm. The practice survived because it bent; the original routine broke.

This distinction—between rhythm and routine—shapes the durability of any spiritual or contemplative life. Routines are brittle.

Once disrupted, they often shatter, dragging guilt behind them. Rhythms, by contrast, follow the deeper cadence of a life in motion. They flex, adjust, and reform without condemnation. That flexibility gestures toward a quieter motif running through this chapter: breath. A breath expands and contracts; it does not accuse. A rhythm behaves likewise. Treating spiritual practice as breath-like—responsive, alive, and cyclical—allows it to accompany shifting responsibilities rather than demand constancy they cannot fulfil.

A rhythm begins with an observable behaviour, not an abstract aspiration. Show the shape of a day. Perhaps mornings are dense with childcare; evenings calmer, or the reverse. Name the point of least resistance. Explain how that moment becomes the anchor for practice. The implication is clear: a rhythm grows from the body's timetable, not the calendar's fantasy. Wilson's pivot from dawn to dusk illustrates this. He did not abandon the deeper intention of steadiness; he changed the hour in which he pursued it. The shift measured only fifteen hours, yet it rescued the practice from extinction.

Historical examples underline this adaptive logic. In 12th-century Kyoto, the Zen master Eisai tailored monastic meditation periods to the agricultural rhythms surrounding his community. Rice planting weeks required shorter formal sittings; harvest days allowed longer sessions. His 1195 reforms at Kennin-ji monastery were controversial precisely because they broke from rigid scheduling, yet the adaptation enabled novices to remain engaged without collapse. Contrast this with the 17th-century Parisian Jansenist convent at Port-Royal, whose harshly regulated routine demanded unvarying prayer hours regardless of health or season. Letters from the period reveal exhaustion and illness among sisters unable to meet the fixed demands. The counter-example stands as a warning: rigidity often masquerades as piety while quietly eroding capacity.

Reconciliation lies in context. Flexible rhythms are not indulgence but design aligned with reality. Neuroscientific studies on behaviour change suggest that adaptability supports long-term consolidation of neural pathways because it reduces the cognitive strain associated with maintenance (Lewis et al., 2019). In lived terms, this looks like a parent shifting practice to nap-time, a nurse meditating after night shifts rather than before, or a student grounding themselves during afternoon lulls instead of idealised dawn sessions. The motif of breath returns: expansion when space opens, contraction when life tightens.

Consider a concrete pattern. Someone who commutes by train between Manchester and Sheffield may use the twenty-minute window after departure to read a reflective paragraph or take ten steady breaths. The visible metric is time: twenty minutes, not perfection. But if their role changes and the commute disappears, clinging to the old routine becomes self-sabotage. A rhythm invites redesign: perhaps using the walk from kitchen to study; perhaps placing a slim book on the dining table for a brief pause before lunch. The context, not the clock, carries the practice.

Guilt is an unhelpful tutor. When routines fracture, guilt often steps in to narrate failure. It mistakes interruption for abandonment. Rhythms neutralise that voice by acknowledging that human lives are seasonal. The philosopher Simone Weil, writing from Marseille in 1941, repeatedly adjusted her personal spiritual disciplines amid wartime dislocation. Her notebooks show short, intense bursts of attention during rare quiet periods, interspersed with weeks of minimal practice. Yet she did not treat the gaps as moral lapses; she viewed them as circumstantial constraints. That perspective freed her to return without self-reproach. Her flexibility resembles Wilson's improvisation: breath, not burden.

Fear of losing progress also fuels rigidity. People cling to routines because they believe deviation erases the neural gains established through repetition. But this fear misreads how memory and habit interact. Old circuits do not disappear immediately during change; they linger, available to re-engage. A short season of adaptation does not undo months of work. The implication is liberating: you can adjust without forfeiting everything. The brain banks previous repetitions as latent competencies. A rhythm, therefore, trusts the residue of practice.

There is a limitation worth acknowledging. Excessive flexibility can dissolve commitment. If practices become endlessly negotiable, they risk fading into good intentions with no gravitational pull. The reconciliation requires a subtle line: flexibility in timing, firmness in intention. The breath expands and contracts, yet always returns. That is the rhythm to emulate. An evening practice may replace a morning one, but the practice itself remains anchored: breathwork, reflection, or prayer continues in a chosen window, however it shifts.

Patterns from different traditions reinforce this guiding principle. In 19th-century Kerala, Hindu householders often adapted temple-based rituals to domestic settings during monsoon seasons when travel became difficult. The offering was shorter, sometimes only a lamp and a mantra, but continuity remained. In early Quaker meetings in England, worship sometimes moved from morning to afternoon during harvest months, recognising agricultural demands. These examples show communities adjusting rhythm without surrendering core commitments. Their wisdom speaks directly to modern practitioners navigating work, family, and care responsibilities.

A rhythm's durability also lies in its emotional tone. Routines often carry implicit pressure: the session must be a certain length; the posture must be correct; the time must be early. A rhythm loosens those demands. It honours the signal rather than the form. If the signal is "pause and return to yourself", then five minutes leaning against the kitchen counter may satisfy the intention better than a meticulously scheduled half-hour at 5:45 a.m. The visible behaviour is brief, grounded presence. It counts.

The motif of breath threads once more. Breath does not shame. It oscillates. It meets the body where the body is. Treating practice—whatever form it takes—as breath-like encourages a compassionate realism. You adapt as conditions change, then re-extend when capacity returns. Rather than guilt, curiosity guides the process. What *works* this week? What expands your awareness rather than crushes it?

All of this leads to an unresolved question that sits at the heart of sustainable spiritual practice. In the next significant shift of your life—be it a new child, a new job, illness, relocation, or care responsibilities—which part of your current practice can bend without breaking? The answer will determine whether your practice lives as a rhythm or fractures as a routine.

Reviewing and Revising Your Path

In November 2014, during his tenure as Master of Magdalene College, Cambridge, the historian Rowan Williams described a moment of disquiet that surprised even him. For years he had begun each morning with a dense theological reading, a practice he considered foundational. Yet one autumn weekend he realised that he had been turning pages without absorption. The habit, once enlivening, had ossified. That Monday he left the book on his desk and walked the college grounds for ten minutes instead. The shift was tiny, barely visible to colleagues, but its effect was immediate: clarity returned, and with it a renewed appetite for the discipline. The practice had not been abandoned; it had been revised. A course correction, modest but decisive, had restored meaning.

That moment captures a pattern familiar to anyone engaged in long-term spiritual work: habits age. What once nourished can become rote. The mind, seeking efficiency, automates practices that require attention. Without periodic scrutiny, even the most sincere commitments risk becoming hollow gestures. Recognising this drift early is not evidence of failure; it signals maturity. Any path worth walking demands review—an honest look at what bears fruit and what has quietly withered. The motif here is the turning page. Sometimes the page must be turned not to continue the same story, but to start a subtly different one.

A meaningful review begins with observation. Show how a practice feels *in the body*. Maybe the breath tightens when you approach a journal. Maybe the prayer that once grounded you now leaves you flat. These micro-signals, when named, help explain the state of your inner landscape. Their implication is practical: you refine based on evidence, not sentimentality. Williams' metric was attention—minutes in which his mind wandered compared with minutes engaged. When the ratio tipped, revision became not optional but wise.

Examples from other traditions reinforce the value of reconsideration. In 13th-century Baghdad, the Sufi scholar Ibn Qayyim al-Jawziyya wrote about the danger of "worship as habit", observing how devotional recitations could lose vitality when repeated without consciousness. His 1341 treatise recommended altering the *form* of remembrance—switching from spoken recitation to silent contemplation or brief prostration—while keeping the intention intact. Centuries earlier, in 6th-century Italy, Benedict of Nursia built review directly into monastic life at Monte Cassino. The Rule of Saint Benedict instructed monks to examine their conduct each evening, not harshly but soberly, adjusting tomorrow's efforts in light of today's truth. Both examples highlight the same principle: revision is not a departure from discipline but its safeguard.

A counter-example shows the cost of ignoring this. In the 20th-century Oxford Group, a Christian movement founded in 1921 and later known as Moral Re-Armament, participants were encouraged to maintain strict daily "quiet time" procedures. While initially energising, the method's uniformity often produced guilt when members struggled to maintain it. Letters from the 1930s reveal participants feeling spiritually defective when their prescribed practices grew stale. This rigidity led some to walk away altogether. The limitation is clear: without room for reflective change, discipline becomes brittle. Reconciliation lies in adopting review as a compassionate practice—watchful, flexible, and honest.

Revising a path requires questions that illuminate rather than accuse. One might ask: *What practice today brings energy rather than depletion? What behaviour yesterday made me more patient? Which habit now feels dutiful but fruitless?* The answers emerge not from grand epiphanies but from attentive noticing. Replace abstractions with observable behaviours: a reading session that yields two lines remembered; a reflective walk that steadies your breath; a moment of silence that softens your tone before a difficult conversation. These tangible metrics anchor revision in reality.

Consider a contemporary scenario. A researcher in Edinburgh may commit to twenty minutes of reading every evening. Over months, she realises she remembers little of what she reads. Her behaviour reveals the truth: her eyes move, but comprehension drops. She switches to a short reflective walk around the block. The change measures ten minutes, yet it yields more clarity than the longer habit. The implication is simple: a shorter, living practice exceeds a longer, lifeless one.

Small revisions compound. A musician in Bristol might find that practising gratitude journalling becomes perfunctory, the entries repetitive. He decides to replace the journal with a single spoken word of thanks when he locks his front door each morning. The behaviour is minimal; the shift in tone noticeable. This is the turning page motif again: a subtle edit, a renewed story.

Yet not all revisions should be immediate. A credible limitation is emotional resistance. Sometimes a practice feels stale not because it has outlived its use, but because one is moving through inner turbulence. Abandoning it too quickly may deprive someone of a stabilising anchor. The reconciliation requires discernment: measure the difference between stagnation and discomfort. Stagnation feels dull; discomfort feels alive, even if challenging. Revision in the former case is growth; persistence in the latter may be necessary training.

Historical models show the nuance. In 17th-century London, diarist Samuel Pepys periodically noted when his spiritual readings felt dull. He alternated between authors—sometimes devotional, sometimes philosophical—to reawaken curiosity. His diaries from 1665 and 1666 show several such shifts. He neither forced the stale text nor abandoned reading altogether. Instead, he adjusted the voice speaking to him.

A rhythm of review prevents drift. Quarterly check-ins work for some; seasonal for others. The frequency matters less than the honesty. Think of these check-ins as calibration points, like a compass held up to a map: small realignments that prevent major misdirection. The behaviour is simple—set aside ten minutes, look at what stirs life, what drains it, what emerges as genuinely fruitful.

The motif of the turning page threads once more. Every revision is a page turned, not a book discarded. Reviewing your path is less about judgement and more about stewardship. You are tending something alive: your attention, your energy, your unfolding self. And tending requires awareness.

This leads to the unresolved question that accompanies every seasoned practitioner: in the next season of your life, which practice deserves renewal, which demands revision, and which—quietly, respectfully—has reached its final page?

Living as Ongoing Experiment

In March 1936, at the Marine Biological Laboratory in Woods Hole, Massachusetts, the geneticist Barbara McClintock recorded a single line in her notebook after weeks of painstaking observation: "*A pattern emerges. Slowly.*" She had been tracing maize chromosomes one cell division at a time, often spending hours at the microscope without clear progress. Yet when she reviewed her notes a year later, she realised how her daily attentiveness had revealed subtle shifts she could not have detected in the moment. That slow accumulation of insight eventually contributed to her Nobel-winning work in 1983. Her patience was not passive. It was experimental, humble, and fiercely curious—the mindset this chapter invites in spiritual practice. McClintock trusted small changes. She watched. She returned. She allowed the evidence of her own experience to teach her.

This spirit—curiosity without haste—captures what it means to live spiritual life as an ongoing experiment. No immediate breakthroughs, no dramatic self-overhauls, no insistence that every session must "work". Instead, one asks: what shifts when I attend gently, daily, and without demanding results? The motif here is the notebook. A year passes. You look back. You see changes you could not have measured day by day.

Spiritual growth often unfolds at a pace quieter than ambition allows. Show an example. A person commits to five minutes of breath meditation each morning. For months the practice feels uneventful. Yet when comparing journal entries from January and December, they notice fewer spikes of irritation during conflict, or a softer tone in conversations they once approached defensively. Name the pattern: neuroplastic consolidation. Explain it: the brain encodes repeated behaviours, even micro-behaviours, into more stable circuits over time, often without conscious fanfare. The implication is profound: consistent experimentation, not perfection, shapes the self.

History offers corroborating examples. In 17th-century Kyoto, the Zen master Bankei Yōtaku taught what he called the "Unborn Mind". His sermons from the 1660s describe spiritual practice not as heroic striving but as steady attention—testing, observing, returning. Bankei refused to prescribe rigid schedules, insisting instead that students watch how their minds responded to conditions and adjust accordingly. A second example comes from 20th-century Paris, where Simone Weil kept a notebook of her daily reflections between 1941 and 1943. Her entries reveal experiments in attention: she tried different ways of anchoring presence in ordinary tasks—washing dishes, queuing for rationed food, copying texts. She evaluated what softened her inner reactivity. These records demonstrate the same principle: experiment, observe, revise.

A limitation must be acknowledged. Not all experimentation feels benign. A person may try several practices—journalling, chanting, mindful walking—only to discover that each initially heightens restlessness. The risk is discouragement, misreading the discomfort as failure. Reconcile this by naming discomfort as part of the data. Early turbulence often indicates that dormant patterns are being stirred. The key is to measure responses over weeks, not minutes. As in McClintock's laboratory, patterns emerge slowly.

Pair every abstraction with behaviour. Curiosity appears in the choice to try a two-minute pause before lunch. Humility appears in acknowledging that yesterday's method did not help. Persistence appears in returning anyway, adjusting variables rather than abandoning the practice. The behaviour is experimental, not devotional perfectionism. The notebook motif returns: each small entry contributes to a larger arc of understanding.

Consider a concrete case. A software engineer in Manchester resolves to reduce evening social media scrolling by five minutes—a micro-intervention. For three weeks, nothing seems to change. But a month later, when reviewing her calendar notes, she notices she has been sleeping ten minutes earlier on average, and her morning mood ratings—she scores them on a simple 1 to 5 scale—improved from a median of 2 to 3. The behaviour is modest; the shift is real. This is spiritual experiment through behavioural data—quiet, honest, and grounded.

Another example: a teacher in Dublin, overwhelmed during exam season, experiments with a brief gratitude phrase whispered during the evening commute. At first it feels contrived. Yet after two months, he realises he no longer ruminates on minor conflicts as intensely. His partner remarks that his tone at home has softened. Again, the notebook pattern: nothing dramatic in the moment, but change visible in retrospect.

The counter-image is the person who treats spiritual life as a test with right and wrong answers. A rigid experimental mindset—where outcomes must conform to preconceived expectations—can narrow growth. The reconciliation lies in returning to genuine inquiry. Instead of "Is this working?" ask "What is this showing?" Instead of "Why is this hard?" ask "What does this hardness reveal?" This shift preserves curiosity while dissolving self-judgement.

Living as experiment also protects against spiritual vanity. If every practice is a test of identity—*Am I a good meditator? Am I progressing fast enough?*—the mind becomes preoccupied with performance. Experiments, by contrast, decentralise the ego. They emphasise conditions, patterns, variables. They welcome surprise. They accept the messiness of data. A difficult week becomes information, not indictment. A lapse becomes a reminder that old circuits remain available. A renewed attempt becomes part of the record, not a heroic restart.

The motif returns again: the notebook. Imagine someone reviewing the past year of their inner life. They notice fewer catastrophic interpretations of silence in relationships. They recall a fraught meeting where they paused before speaking. They see how an old resentment has loosened, not through dramatic forgiveness but through repeated micro-choices to breathe rather than tighten.

These are signs of rewiring—subtle, durable, and easily missed unless one looks.

Scientific parallels support this framing. In 2005, researchers at University College London documented the gradual thickening of grey matter in London taxi drivers as they acquired spatial knowledge. The changes were not immediate; they emerged over years. Though unrelated to spiritual practice, the study illustrates a shared principle: repeated engagement shapes the brain in increments, not leaps. The spiritual path, like navigation through a complex city, is learned through exposure, reflection, and ongoing adjustment.

A further implication is that experiments need constraints. A good scientist defines variables. A practitioner might commit to a single change for a set period—six weeks, twelve weeks—and observe without judging. This protects against impulsive oscillation between methods. It also nurtures humility: you commit to learning, not to perfection.

A final scene grounds the principle. A person sits at their desk in Bristol at year's end, reviewing a small notebook kept with irregular discipline. The entries are brief: "Snapped less at work." "Listened longer to Mum." "Walked instead of scrolled." No fireworks. Yet taken together, the notes sketch a life gently redirected. The experiment is working, not through grandeur but through quiet constancy.

This leads to the unresolved question that gives momentum to the practice: in the coming year, what single variable—tiny, human, measurable—are you willing to adjust, observe, and learn from without demanding immediate transformation?

About the Author

Aisha Calderon writes from the meeting point of inner work and everyday life. Over many years of personal practice and teaching, she has explored how simple disciplines of attention, compassion, and gratitude change the felt texture of ordinary days. Her work is shaped by a respect for both neuroscience and ancient wisdom, without forcing either into neat agreement. Raised between cultures, she is especially interested in how stories about the self are carried, healed, and renewed across generations. Aisha's writing invites readers into spiritual practice that is steady rather than showy, rooted in the realities of family, work, and community. Her central conviction is modest but demanding: that the brain's plasticity is an opportunity, and that, with patience, our inner wiring can better reflect the courage, clarity, and kindness we most admire.

www.ingramcontent.com/pod-product-compliance
Lightning Source LLC
Chambersburg PA
CBHW031344230926
51848CB00002B/382
* 9 7 8 9 3 7 5 3 6 9 4 5 5 *